BIBLE STUDY GUIDE

From the Bible-teaching ministry of

Charles R. Swindoll

INSIGHT FOR LIVING

Charles R. Swindoll is a graduate of Dallas Theological Seminary and has served in pastorates in Texas, Massachusetts, and California since 1963. He has served as senior pastor of the First Evangelical Free Church of Fullerton, California, since 1971. Chuck's radio program, "Insight for Living," began in 1979. In addition to his church and radio ministries, Chuck enjoys writing. He has authored numerous books and booklets on a variety of subjects.

Based on the outlines and transcripts of Chuck's sermons, the study guide text is co-authored by Lee Hough, a graduate of The University of Texas at Arlington and Dallas Theological Seminary.

Editor in Chief:	**Typographer:**
Cynthia Swindoll	Bob Haskins
Coauthor of Text:	**Director, Communications Division:**
Lee Hough	Carla Meberg
Assistant Editor:	**Project Manager:**
Wendy Peterson	Alene Cooper
Copyediting Supervisor:	**Project Coordinator:**
Marty Anderson	Carolyn Roberts
Copy Editor:	**Print Production Manager:**
Marty Anderson	Deedee Snyder
Designer:	**Assistant Production Manager:**
Gary Lett	John Norton
Production Artists:	**Printer:**
Gary Lett and Robert McGuire	Frye and Smith

Unless otherwise identified, all Scripture references are from the New American Standard Bible, © The Lockman Foundation 1960, 1962, 1963, 1968, 1971, 1972, 1973, 1975, 1977. Used by permission.

Scripture taken from the Holy Bible, New International Version, Copyright © 1973, 1978, 1984 International Bible Society, used by permission of Zondervan Bible Publishers.

Scripture marked [KJV] is taken from the King James Version of the Bible.

An effort has been made to locate sources and obtain permission where necessary for the quotations used in this book. In the event of any unintentional omission, a modification will gladly be incorporated in future printings.

ISBN 0-8499-8421-1

Printed in the United States of America.

COVER: photograph by G. Robert Nease, calligraphy by A. Egan Healy.

CONTENTS

INTRODUCTION

"Incarnate the Truth!"

I can still hear one of my favorite seminary profs saying that. And I have repeated it on numerous occasions myself. It is a helpful and accurate statement. Abstract truth seems sterile and difficult to grasp if it stands alone—but when we see it illustrated in a life, it's amazing how clearly it emerges and how attainable it becomes. This, of course, is the genius behind any biography.

Joseph is a classic example. He embodies some of the most significant truths in all of Scripture. Although a man just like us, Joseph blazes a new trail through a jungle of mistreatment, false accusations, *undeserved* punishment, and gross misunderstanding. He exemplifies forgiveness, freedom from bitterness, and an unbelievably positive attitude toward those who had done him harm. From one episode to the next, you will literally shake your head in amazement.

That's the way it is when mere humanity incarnates divine truth. My prayer is that this principle will not stop with Joseph.

Chuck Swindoll

Chuck Swindoll

PUTTING TRUTH INTO ACTION

Knowledge apart from application falls short of God's desire for His children. He wants us to apply what we learn so that we will change and grow. This study guide was prepared with these goals in mind. As you go through the following pages, we hope your desire to discover biblical truth will grow as your understanding of God's Word increases, and that you will be encouraged to apply what you've learned.

To assist you in your study, we've included a section called **Living Insights** at the end of each lesson. These exercises will challenge you to study further and to think of specific ways to put your discoveries into action.

There are many ways to use this guide—in personal devotions, group studies, discussions with friends and family, and Sunday school classes. And, of course, it's an ideal study aid when you're listening to its corresponding "Insight for Living" radio series.

To benefit most from this study guide, we would encourage you to consider it a spiritual journal. That's why we've included space in the **Living Insights** for recording your thoughts and discoveries. We hope you'll return to those sections often for review and encouragement as you continue to grow in your walk with Christ.

Lee Hough
Coauthor of Text

Chapter 1

FAVORED SON, HATED BROTHER

Genesis 37

Reading the Bible is sometimes like sitting on one of those wide front porches your grandparents used to have. The kind where you had a porch-swing view of the whole neighborhood. Only from the Bible's inspired veranda, your view stretches from an earth under construction at one end of the block all the way to the shiny streets of a new heaven and earth at the other.

Quite a view. And there are lots of neighbors too. If you look off in the direction of Genesis, you can see Adam working up a sweat, or Noah stocking a boat, or two old timers—Abraham and Sarah—out promenading their little baby Isaac. A couple of books up from those folks live David and his best friend Jonathan. Just a stone's throw from them lives an important fellow named Nehemiah who is cupbearer to King Artaxerxes. And next door to him is Esther—she's being raised by her cousin Mordecai.

You'd probably be surprised at how many Christians have never taken the time to come down from the New Testament side of the street to meet some of their Old Testament neighbors. That's what we want to do in this study—take you down the block to the first book in the Bible and introduce you to an unforgettable fellow. Someone whose biography occupies more space in Genesis than Adam, Noah, Abraham, or even his own father, Jacob. Someone who responded to broken dreams and impossible circumstances with a faith that propelled him from the pit of slavery to the pinnacle of respect.

The fellow, whose doorstep we'll be camping on, is Joseph. He had quite an unusual life. One that the apostle Paul guaranteed

1

would instruct you on how to live, offer you encouragement, and provide you with warnings and timely reproofs (compare Rom. 15:4, 1 Cor. 10:11, 2 Tim. 3:16–17).

If you're ready, let's walk down the street and meet this young man who was the favorite of his father but the hated brother of his siblings.

A Brief Overview

Before we are formally introduced to Joseph, let's gather some brief background information, looking specifically at three distinct segments of his biography.

Birth to age seventeen (Gen. 30:24–37:2): If Joseph's life were a storm, this period would be the clouds swelling up to eclipse the sun. The family is in transition, unsettled, moving. A growing sense of agitation is in the wind. You can hear the low rumblings of pain and discontent building as his family clashes over jealousies, lust, and hatred.

Seventeen to age thirty (37:2–41:46): As Joseph enters into young manhood, the brewing storm finally bursts and rejection, enslavement, and imprisonment rain down on him.

Thirty to death (41:46–50:26): The last eighty years of Joseph's life are years of prosperity under God's blessing. It was a perfect opportunity for Joseph to exact revenge on his brothers, to blot out the sun from their lives, but he blesses and brightens their lives instead.

Setting the Stage

Now that we have a feel for the overall direction of Joseph's life, let's go back to the beginning and see how it all started.

The home in which Joseph grew up was anything but a place of refuge or shelter. It was, instead, the eye of a storm. And the front door that lets us in to this turbulent biography is found in Genesis 37.

This chapter introduces you to the middle section of Joseph's life and works forward from there. The first person you encounter, however, and need to understand is Joseph's father, Jacob. His other name, given later in life by God, is Israel, meaning "prince with God." It was a tremendous improvement over his original name, which meant "chiseler."

Jacob: The Aging Father

From his earliest years Jacob had a knack for living up to his first name. He cheated and lied his way along, and except for a few brief interludes of piety, he couldn't be trusted.

Another unstable area that plagued Jacob's family were his marriages. He had two wives who were sisters, Leah and Rachel, but Rachel was the one he loved. This set up a rivalry that resulted in a childbearing competition.

Leah was the first to have children, and she eventually produced seven, six boys and a girl named Dinah. Rachel, however, was barren—a disgrace for a woman in those times. So she had her handmaiden, Bilhah, sleep with Jacob so that she might have children through her. Bilhah eventually bore Jacob two sons. Not to be outdone, Leah retaliated by having her handmaiden, Zilpah, lay with Jacob, and she bore him two sons also (Gen. 29–30). Finally, Rachel herself bore a child, and she named him Joseph (30:22–24).[1]

Add all this up and you've got one husband, two wives, two concubines, four mothers, eleven sons, and one daughter—which did not equal marital bliss. Instead, there were jealousy, strife, anger, lust, deceit, competition, and secrecy.

By this time Jacob was no longer a young man. He'd worked for his father-in-law, Laban, a total of twenty years, and there had been a lot of family infighting and deception on the part of both father-in-law and son-in-law. So Jacob decided to move his family back to Canaan, his homeland (v. 25).

Canaan: The Promised Land

The trip home came to an abrupt halt, however, when the family reached the land of the Hivites and the city of Shechem. There Jacob and Leah's daughter was raped (34:1–2).

Incredibly, when Jacob heard of the despicable act, he did nothing. But her brothers did. They quickly devised a way to deceive the Hivites and then proceeded to kill every male and loot their city (vv. 4–29). When Jacob finally did voice a concern over the situation, it wasn't about the welfare of his daughter. He was concerned about his public image among the surrounding peoples (vv. 30–31).

---

1. Joseph means "May He add." It was an expression of Rachel's hope that God would give her another son.

3

So the family moved on, but it wasn't long before a second tragedy struck. While en route to the next city, Jacob's beloved Rachel died giving birth to their second child, Joseph's brother Benjamin (35:16–18).

Jacob had worked fourteen years to marry Rachel. They had waited long for Joseph to be born. And now, after another long wait, Benjamin was born, but at the expense of the one woman whom Jacob had truly loved.

After the funeral the family moved on again—right into a third tragic situation: Reuben, the oldest son, committed incest with one of his father's concubines (v. 22a).

The text clearly states that Jacob heard about it. But, just as when his daughter was raped, he did nothing. Jacob just let things go on as if nothing had happened.[2]

What started out as an exciting trip home ended up being a gauntlet of grief. The final blow came after Jacob reached Canaan, when his father, Isaac, died (35:27–29).

Joseph: The Favorite Son

Jacob's arrival in Canaan brings us back to Genesis 37 and the front door of Joseph's biography. The clouds hanging over Joseph's family at this juncture in his life were like dark bruises, swollen with the pain of years of unresolved conflicts. Yet in the midst of all this, Jacob discovered an oasis, a shelter against the turbulence he felt within the rest of his family.

> Now Israel [Jacob] loved Joseph more than all his sons, because he was the son of his old age. (v. 3a)

Doting on Joseph may have brightened Jacob's world, but it brought only dark clouds into Joseph's. And Joseph's own tattling on his brothers in verse 2 did nothing to dispel those clouds.
Then there was the matter of a certain coat.

The Brothers: Jealous Conflict

> And Israel made [Joseph] a varicolored tunic. And his brothers saw that their father loved him more than all his brothers; and so they hated him and could not speak to him on friendly terms. (vv. 3b–4)

---

2. Jacob may have acted as if nothing had happened, but he knew his son had committed a great sin and he never forgot it. Years later, when this passive father lay on his deathbed, he finally did address the evil that had been done (see Gen. 49:1–4).

This tunic was more than a simple gift from a loving father. It was a long-sleeved garment worn by the nobility of the day, a symbol of authority and favored position within the family.[3] And the rest of the boys jealously hated Joseph for it.

That hatred dug in a little deeper when Joseph related a dream to his brothers in which he became their ruler (vv. 5–8). Then Joseph told another dream, this time with Jacob listening, where again everyone in the family was bowing down to him (vv. 9–11). Jacob wasn't too fond of Joseph's words, but still he did nothing to assuage the ill feelings that were driving a wedge between Joseph and his brothers. He simply "kept the saying in mind" (v. 11) and ignored the thundering signs of the oncoming storm.

A Plan to Kill Joseph

> "When it is evening, you say, 'It will be fair weather, for the sky is red.' And in the morning, 'There will be a storm today, for the sky is red and threatening.' Do you know how to discern the appearance of the sky, but cannot discern the signs of the times?" (Matt. 16:2–3)

Jesus was speaking to the Pharisees and Sadducees, but he could just as well have been speaking to Jacob.

Sent by Father

Like any good shepherd, Jacob knew how to discern the appearance of the sky. But he chose to ignore the red, threatening signs that hung over his own family. He didn't see the danger in sending Joseph to check up on his brothers, who were pasturing the family's flock in Shechem (Gen. 37:12–17).

Mistreated by Brothers

When Joseph finally spotted his brothers with the flock, they were in Dothan, twenty miles north of Shechem. Twenty miles north of the city where those same brothers had slaughtered every male out of rage over their sister's rape.

---

3. "Jacob presented Joseph with a coat of many colours (KJV), or a coat with long sleeves, which set him in a class apart and exempted him from the menial tasks of farming." Joyce G. Baldwin, *The Message of Genesis 12–50: From Abraham to Joseph*, The Bible Speaks Today series (Downers Grove, Ill.: InterVarsity Press, 1986), p. 159.

When the brothers saw Joseph coming, they immediately held a family council. The time had come to vent their wrath again, just as they had done in Shechem. The only question to be settled was how.

> When they saw him from a distance and before he came close to them, they plotted against him to put him to death. . . . "Now then, come and let us kill him and throw him into one of the pits; and we will say, 'A wild beast devoured him.'" (vv. 18, 20a)

Reuben, however, interceded on Joseph's behalf and persuaded the others to put him in a pit instead of killing him outright. When Joseph arrived, they stripped him of the coat Jacob had given him, threw him in a pit, and coolly sat down to eat (vv. 21–25a).

A Caravan to Egypt

While they were eating, the brothers decided to sell him to a passing caravan of Ishmaelites. Next, they poured goat's blood on Joseph's tunic, and when they got home they deceived their father into thinking Joseph was killed by a wild animal. Jacob wept bitterly (vv. 25b–35).

In a way, all the things Jacob had been too passive and preoccupied to deal with in the past finally crashed in on him. Behind the cruel and deceitful actions of his sons lay many accusing questions. Where were you, Jacob, when Dinah was raped? when your sons slaughtered the men in Shechem? when Reuben committed incest? when the whole family was being torn apart by jealousy and anger?

As the shepherd of a large family, Jacob had refused to see or do anything about the red sky warnings that had spread over his flock. He had let his children sow the wind, until they reaped a whirlwind (see Hos. 8:7).

Meanwhile, Joseph was taken into Egypt and sold as a slave to the captain of the guard in Pharaoh's court (Gen. 37:36).

Four Lessons to Be Learned

Imagine your own family tossing you into a pit to die, then sitting down for dinner. Imagine being sold as a slave, taken to a country you didn't know, to be owned by a man you'd never seen. And all this while you were only seventeen years old!

All we can do is imagine. However, there are four lessons we can glean from Joseph's experience that can be just as important and real for us today as they were for Joseph.

First: *No family is exempt from adversity.* There is no place of refuge in this fallen world where one can escape trials. There is only One who can give you the refuge and strength to endure and grow through them (see Ps. 46).

Second: *No enemy is more subtle than passivity.* Do you know how passive parents tend to discipline? Usually in anger. For weeks, months, even years, these individuals try to avoid dealing with problems until one day they explode. And in a brutal moment they'll come down on someone with both feet. But that isn't discipline. The child they leave behind after one of these scorching sessions will be no more disciplined than before. We've got to realize that giving in to the subtle urge to avoid problems now only creates more in the future.

Third: *No response is more cruel than jealousy.* Solomon was right when he said that jealousy is as cruel as the grave (Song of Sol. 8:6, KJV). If you let the seed of jealousy take root in your children, it will destroy the family's unity and harmony. As a parent, you must learn to recognize and weed out bad attitudes as well as actions. And in addition to your weeding responsibilities, don't forget to water your children with praise when they display the right attitudes.

Fourth: *No condition is more unfair than slavery.* In one day Joseph went from a favored son to a faceless slave, from luxury's pillows to Egypt's bonds. No one in Joseph's family knew where he ended up, not even the brothers who sold him. But God knew where he was. And no amount of unfair circumstances could thwart His plan to raise Joseph from pit to pinnacle.

 Living Insights

We all have memories from our childhood. They're like pictures, living photographs that linger on even after our parents have died.

In his book *The Gift of Remembrance,* author Ken Gire reminisces on three pictures of growing up with his father. One of those pictures, taken thirty years, twelve hundred miles, and a wife and four kids ago, was the remembrance of his father treating a mentally disabled boy with dignity and kindness. A memory that continues to shape the destiny of his own life.

I found that when I wrote my first book,
   it was about a mentally disabled boy.
When I did volunteer work,
   it was with the handicapped.
And every time I encounter those who are
   in some way bent or broken,
   my heart softens.
I send up a little prayer—
   that the load they carry
   may be made easier to bear,
   that they may be protected
   from the cruelties of this world,
   and that they may experience as much
   as they can of the goodness
   life has to offer.[4]

From our study today, what pictures of their father do you think Jacob's sons and daughter carried with them throughout their lives?

_____

_____

_____

_____

In the time that it will take to finish this study on Joseph's life, what lasting, good memories can you give to your children or to other children you know?

_____

_____

_____

_____

_____

4. Ken Gire, *The Gift of Remembrance* (Grand Rapids, Mich.: Zondervan Publishing House, Daybreak Books, 1990), p. 23.

What pictures will *my* son remember
when he comes to the plain granite marker
over *his* father's grave?
What will my daughters remember?
Or my wife?

What pictures will be left behind
for them to thumb through
in the nostalgic, late afternoons
of their lives?

Will the pictures strengthen them for the journey?
Or send them hobbling through life, crippled.[5]

 ## *Living Insights*

In his book *How to Really Love Your Child,* Dr. Ross Campbell
asserts,

> The husband who will take full, total, overall re-
> sponsibility for his family, and take the initiative in
> conveying his love to his wife and children, will
> experience unbelievable rewards: a loving, apprecia-
> tive, helping wife who will be her loveliest for him;
> children who are safe, secure, content and able to
> grow to be their best. I personally have never seen
> marriage fail if these priorities are met. Every failing
> marriage I have seen has somehow missed these pri-
> orities. Fathers, the initiative must be ours.[6]

Jacob didn't take the initiative with his family—and it showed.
Instead of providing an atmosphere where his children could grow
to do and be their best, Jacob's passivity fostered a family environ-
ment that all but guaranteed they would turn out reckless, insecure,
and discontented.

Dads, are you taking the initiative to convey to your children, in
ways they can understand, that they are loved unconditionally? Pause

---

5. Gire, *The Gift of Remembrance,* p. 51.

6. D. Ross Campbell, *How to Really Love Your Child* (Wheaton, Ill.: SP Publications, Victor
Books, 1977), p. 23.

9

for a moment and take inventory of what you're currently practicing. (Moms, why don't you do this too!)

_____

_____

_____

_____

_____

_____

_____

_____

_____

Now spend some time with your spouse brainstorming some new ways for you to effectively convey your love.

_____

_____

_____

_____

_____

_____

_____

_____

_____

If you need help, try reading *How to Really Love Your Child* by Dr. Ross Campbell, or *Traits of a Healthy Family* by Dolores Curran, or *How Do You Say, "I Love You"?* by Judson J. Swihart.

Chapter 2
RESISTING TEMPTATION
Genesis 39

In one of his best writings, a small booklet fewer than fifty pages long titled *Temptation*, Dietrich Bonhoeffer gave perhaps the single most descriptive explanation of temptation anywhere outside the Scriptures.

> In our members there is a slumbering inclination towards desire which is both sudden and fierce. With irresistible power, desire seizes mastery over the flesh. All at once a secret, smouldering fire is kindled. The flesh burns and is in flames. It makes no difference whether it is sexual desire, or ambition, or vanity, or desire for revenge, or love of fame and power, or greed for money or, finally, that strange desire for the beauty of the world, of nature. Joy in God is in course of being extinguished in us and we seek all our joy in the creature. At this moment God is quite unreal to us, he loses all reality, and only desire for the creature is real; the only reality is the devil. Satan does not here fill us with hatred of God, but with forgetfulness of God. . . . The lust thus aroused envelops the mind and will of man in deepest darkness. The powers of clear discrimination and of decision are taken from us. . . .
>
> It is here that everything within me rises up against the Word of God.[1]

Temptation is the oldest of all the inner conflicts in the heart of man. There is not one person, including Christ, who hasn't struggled with it. And, except for Christ, there is not one person who hasn't suffered the consequences of yielding to it.

---

1. Dietrich Bonhoeffer, *Creation and Fall* and *Temptation* (New York, N.Y.: Macmillan Publishing Co., Collier Books, 1959), pp. 116–17.

Three Types of Temptation

Whenever the subject of temptation comes up, people tend to assume that we're talking about sexual lust. But there are other ways we can be tempted.

Material temptation. This is a lust for things. It can be something as large as a house or as small as a ring. Something as bright and dazzling as a new car or as faded and nicked as an antique bureau.

Personal temptation. This is a lust for status. Some people expend all their energies trying to gain special recognition, fame, or power. They sacrifice friends, family—whatever gets in their way—to possess a title or a position.

Sensual temptation. This is the lust for another person. It's the desire to enjoy the body of another individual when such pleasure is not legally or morally permissible.

Regardless of the kind of temptation, all of us know the frustration of trying to stop a Gulliver lust with a Lilliputian will.

In our lesson today we're going to look at Joseph's memorable example and see how he resisted the seductive enticements of a sensual temptation.

The Historic Situation

> Now Joseph had been taken down to Egypt; and Potiphar, an Egyptian officer of Pharaoh, the captain of the bodyguard, bought him from the Ishmaelites, who had taken him down there. And the Lord was with Joseph, so he became a successful man. And he was in the house of his master, the Egyptian. (Gen. 39:1–2)

In the first two verses, two things are conspicuous by their absence. First, there's no mention of how long Joseph had been Potiphar's slave before the events in this chapter took place. He could have been there a few months or a few years; we're not told.

Second, there's no mention of the difficult adjustments Joseph must have had to make as a slave in a foreign land and culture. Remember, he was used to a doting old father and privileges that exempted him from menial tasks. Now he had to obey the commands of Pharaoh's chief executioner and do his menial tasks.

But God's blessing was on Joseph's life and this, coupled with Joseph's personal integrity and hard work, led to his being promoted to a place of prominence.

> Now his master saw that the Lord was with him and
> how the Lord caused all that he did to prosper in
> his hand. So Joseph found favor in his sight, and
> became his personal servant; and he made him over-
> seer over his house, and all that he owned he put
> in his charge. (vv. 3–4)

Notice that Joseph didn't *tell* Potiphar that the Lord was with
him; verse 3 says, "his master saw" that God was with him. And
verse 4 says, "Joseph found favor in his [Potiphar's] sight," not
"Joseph requested favors from Potiphar." Joseph earned the right to
be respected and trusted.

> And it came about that from the time he made him
> overseer in his house, and over all that he owned,
> the Lord blessed the Egyptian's house on account of
> Joseph; thus the Lord's blessing was upon all that he
> owned, in the house and in the field. So he left
> everything he owned in Joseph's charge; and with
> him there he did not concern himself with anything
> except the food which he ate. (vv. 5–6a)

By now, Joseph's Midas touch and personal integrity had inspired
Potiphar's absolute confidence and trust. And along with that had
come greater measures of responsibility and freedom for Joseph. But
sneaking up behind these benefits also came a greater measure of
vulnerability. F. B. Meyer warns,

> *We may expect temptation in days of prosperity and
> ease* rather than in those of privation and toil . . .
> not where men frown, but where they smile sweet,
> exquisite smiles of flattery—it is *there*, it is *there*,
> that the temptress lies in wait! Beware! If thou goest
> armed anywhere, thou must, above all, go armed
> here.[2]

The writer of Genesis finished this brief narrative of Joseph's
professional life with a personal aside: "Now Joseph was handsome
in form and appearance" (v. 6b).

---

2. F. B. Meyer, *Joseph: Beloved—Hated—Exalted* (Fort Washington, Pa.: Christian Literature
Crusade, n.d.), p. 30.

The Sensual Temptation

While Mr. Potiphar is appreciating Joseph's reliable business sense and trustworthy nature, Mrs. Potiphar is becoming increasingly preoccupied with Joseph's good build and looks.

> And it came about after these events that his master's wife looked with desire at Joseph, and she said, "Lie with me." (v. 7)

Joseph immediately but politely refuses. He tries to appeal first to her reason and second to her conscience.

> But he refused and said to his master's wife, "Behold, with me here, my master does not concern himself with anything in the house, and he has put all that he owns in my charge. There is no one greater in this house than I, and he has withheld nothing from me except you, because you are his wife. How then could I do this great evil, and sin against God?" (vv. 8–9)

But Mrs. Potiphar isn't moved a bit. She isn't interested in the sanctity of her marriage or the trust between her husband and Joseph. She's interested only in gratifying her physical lust—*now.* Nothing else. It's no wonder, then, that Joseph's spiritual concern could not penetrate the darkness that shrouded her mind and will.

Peculiar Elements in Joseph's Temptation

Let's pause for just a moment to clarify some of the specifics in Joseph's situation. First, Joseph faced a difficult dilemma. The very place in which he lived and worked, Potiphar's household, brought him face-to-face with one very seductive temptation, Mrs. Potiphar. Second, her advances surely must have flattered Joseph's ego and aroused a powerful sensual temptation. Third, the source of temptation was persistent—she pursued him day after day (v. 10). Fourth, this woman pursued Joseph when they were alone, when there wouldn't be any fear of detection (v. 11).

It was a vulnerable time for Joseph. No doubt his own lust was working overtime trying to erode, as Bonhoeffer said, his powers of clear discrimination and decision (see also James 1:13–15).

The final test for Joseph came when Mrs. Potiphar resorted to more than just words to lure him to lie with her.

And she caught him by his garment, saying, "Lie with me!" And he left his garment in her hand and fled, and went outside. (Gen. 39:12)

In almost every instance where the issue of sexual lust is dealt with in the New Testament, we're told to flee, to get up and run (see 1 Cor. 6:18). Some temptations we're to stand and resist. But when it comes to sensual lust, we're told to do exactly as Joseph did—get out of there. If we stay, we're likely to give in.

The Personal Ramifications

William Congreve once said, "Heaven has no rage like love to hatred turned, Nor hell a fury like a woman scorned."[3] All the lust that had smoldered in Potiphar's wife suddenly blazed into fury. She wanted revenge for her rejection.

So she left his garment beside her until his master came home. Then she spoke to him with these words, "The Hebrew slave, whom you brought to us, came in to me to make sport of me; and it happened as I raised my voice and screamed, that he left his garment beside me and fled outside."

Now it came about when his master heard the words of his wife, which she spoke to him, saying, "This is what your slave did to me," that his anger burned. So Joseph's master took him and put him into the jail, the place where the king's prisoners were confined; and he was there in the jail. (Gen. 39:16–20)

Joseph did the right thing. But once he got outside, he didn't hear any angels singing his praises for saying no. What he heard instead was the scream of a woman—a scream that would hurl him from the heights as Potiphar's overseer to the depths of an obscure jail cell.[4]

---

3. *Bartlett's Familiar Quotations*, 15th ed., rev. and enl., ed. Emily Morison Beck (Boston, Mass.: Little, Brown and Co., 1980), p. 324.

4. At first glance, Potiphar's reaction to his wife's story seems to indicate that he believed her. But when you read of Joseph's punishment, it suggests that his Egyptian master wasn't completely convinced. The normal sentence for a slave guilty of attempted rape was instant death. But Pharaoh's chief executioner kept his sword sheathed and put Joseph in prison instead.

Practical Application for Today

Here are four important insights to help you say no when your lust says yes.

Do not be weakened by your situation. Several aspects of Joseph's position could easily have undercut his resolve to say no to lust. He was handsome and alone. He enjoyed a secure and trusted position. His integrity and accomplishments made him the object of much praise. And, perhaps, most dangerously, he had complete autonomy. He was accountable to no one. No one, that is, except God. Joseph did not allow his eyes to wander from his holy God to the sinful seductions of his situation.

Do not be deceived by persuasion. Mrs. Potiphar was bold, calculating, and her proposition was tantalizing. No doubt her verbal enticements were as loosely clad and suggestive as she probably was. Day after day she tried to lure Joseph with just the right combination of tempting words, such as, "My husband doesn't meet my needs." Or "Who will ever find out? We're completely safe!" Or perhaps "Just this once. Never, never again." But her words were in vain. Joseph's commitment to God completely shut her out.

Do not be gentle with your emotions. F. B. Meyer said, "Resist the first tiny thrill of temptation, lest it widen a breach big enough to admit the ocean. Remember that no temptation can master you unless you admit it *within.*"[5] Our emotions will beg and plead for us to open the door to that first tiny thrill of temptation, but we've got to learn to keep the door closed like Joseph did. In verse 8 "he refused." In verse 9 he calls her words "this great evil, and a sin against God." In verse 10 he didn't even listen to her or be with her. And in verse 12 he fled from her!

Do not be confused by the immediate results. Don't be confused when your "Mrs. Potiphars" keep coming back to tempt you after you've said no. Saying no to temptation, whatever kind it may be, doesn't banish it forever. Lust doesn't give up that easily. Be prepared to say no again the next day—or even the next minute.

 ## Living Insights   STUDY ONE

Even with these helpful insights, many of us are still going to give in to lust. And that's because of one basic problem. Jerry Bridges discovered this problem in his study of 1 John 2.

5. Meyer, *Joseph,* p. 34.

16

One day as I was studying this chapter I realized that my personal life's objective regarding holiness was less than that of John's. He was saying, in effect, "Make it your aim *not* to sin." As I thought about this, I realized that deep within my heart my real aim was not to sin *very much.* . . .

Can you imagine a soldier going into battle with the aim of "not getting hit very much"? . . . We can be sure if that is our aim, we will be hit—not with bullets, but with temptation over and over again.[6]

The battle of saying no to lust is really won or lost in our attitude toward sin. Before you walk onto the spiritual battlefield today, do two things. First, be sure to equip yourself with the four helpful insights given above. And second, think through the three categories of temptation listed and ask yourself this one, decisive question, Has my battle plan been not to sin very much . . . or not to sin at all, in the area of:

material temptations? _____

personal temptations? _____

sensual temptations? _____

 ## *Living Insights*

Listen again to Jerry Bridges, as he shares some insights that help explain the battle we feel going on inside us each time we're tempted.

Desire has come to be the strongest faculty of man's heart. The next time you face one of your typical temptations, watch for the struggle between your desires and your reason. If you give in to temptation, it will be because desire has overcome reason in the struggle to influence your will. . . .

. . . If we are to win this battle for holiness, we must recognize that the basic problem lies within us. It is our own evil desires that lead us into tempta-

6. Jerry Bridges, *The Pursuit of Holiness* (Colorado Springs, Colo.: NavPress, 1978), p. 96.

tion. We may think we merely respond to outward temptations that are presented to us. But the truth is, our evil desires are constantly searching out temptations to satisfy their insatiable lusts.[7]

All of us have weaknesses that allow certain temptations to get through our defenses and take control of our hearts. Fortunately for Joseph, none of his circumstances were able to overcome his commitment to saying no. Are any of the circumstances that he faced difficult for you?

_____

_____

Think through each category and list the circumstances you need to avoid so you don't fall into temptation's trap.

Material: _____

_____

_____

_____

_____

Personal: _____

_____

_____

_____

Sensual: _____

_____

_____

_____

_____

7. Bridges, *The Pursuit of Holiness*, p. 66.

Chapter 3

IMPRISONED AND FORGOTTEN BY MAN

Genesis 39:20–41:1

Alexander Solzhenitsyn and Elie Wiesel. Both men represent millions of other men, women, and children who have been imprisoned and forgotten by man. People who suffered unjustly in Russian gulags or Nazi concentration camps. For some, like Solzhenitsyn, these man-made hells helped bring about their spiritual conversion. For others, like Wiesel, the hellish experience reduced what faith they had to a scorched cinder.

> Never shall I forget that night, the first night in camp, which has turned my life into one long night, seven times cursed and seven times sealed. Never shall I forget that smoke. Never shall I forget the little faces of the children, whose bodies I saw turned into wreaths of smoke beneath a silent blue sky.
> Never shall I forget those flames which consumed my faith forever.
> Never shall I forget that nocturnal silence which deprived me, for all eternity, of the desire to live. Never shall I forget those moments which murdered my God and my soul and turned my dreams to dust. Never shall I forget these things, even if I am condemned to live as long as God Himself. Never.[1]

The pain of suffering unjustly is one of the severest trials we can enter into. It is a sanctuary of flames from which some emerge with a tempered, unshakable faith; while others, only ashes.

It is also inescapable. Every day children are stolen, abused, and aborted. Wives are battered. Spouses are abandoned by unfaithful partners. Drunk drivers maim and kill. Gossip and slander ruin reputations.

---

1. Elie Wiesel, *Night,* trans. Stella Rodway (New York, N.Y.: Bantam Books, 1960), p. 32.

The greatest test in this kind of suffering is our attitude toward it. Viktor Frankl wrote,

> Everything can be taken from a man but one thing: the last of the human freedoms—to choose one's attitude in any given set of circumstances, to choose one's own way.[2]

We cannot control whether today or tomorrow we will be treated fairly. But we can choose how we will respond. Our attitude is something we can control. Resentment, hostility, bitterness, revenge— these are the common attitudes people choose when they're mistreated. God, however, has a different choice in mind for His children.

> For what credit is there if, when you sin and are harshly treated, you endure it with patience? But if when you do what is right and suffer for it you patiently endure it, this finds favor with God. (1 Pet. 2:20)

Joseph did what was right and he suffered for it. He refused Mrs. Potiphar's advances, so she concocted a lie that sent him to prison. From free man to slave to prisoner, Joseph's freedom was progressively stripped away. Everything about his circumstances seemed to indicate that he had been forgotten by both God and man. Now Joseph faced the most difficult part of being mistreated unfairly. Now he had to exercise the only freedom left to him—the freedom to choose his attitude.

Before we see how Joseph responded, let's take a brief look at the different ways we all suffer unjustly.

Mistreatment: Common to Everyone

We all experience, basically, three kinds of mistreatment:

Undeserved treatment from family. Even in the best of families you won't escape pain, because parents aren't perfect and neither are brothers and sisters.

Unexpected restrictions from circumstances. Mistreatment confines us either physically or emotionally. We may be in a situation where we can't fight back or change things. And these unexpected restrictions are painful.

2. Viktor E. Frankl, *Man's Search for Meaning*, rev. and updated (New York, N.Y.: Pocket Books, 1984), p. 86.

Untrue accusations from people. James aptly describes the tongue as a fire (James 3:5–6). In one day its careless, untrue statements can completely incinerate a reputation that has taken years to build.

Imprisonment: Joseph in Jail

If you've ever wondered whether the Bible deals with real life situations, the story of Joseph should dispel any doubts. We've only studied two chapters in his biography so far, and already he has experienced all three categories of mistreatment: his brothers hated him and sold him into slavery; he was confined as someone else's slave; and he was falsely accused by his master's wife. Once again Joseph was thrown from a privileged position into a pit—only this time, instead of a dry well in Dothan, it was a dark dungeon in Egypt (Gen. 39:20).

Where Was God in All of This?

It's usually easy to see God in the good things that happen to us. But what about when something unfair happens, like Joseph being thrown into prison—where was God then? Genesis 39:21 tells us, "The Lord was with Joseph." He never left him. Furthermore, the Lord

> extended kindness to him, and gave him favor in
> the sight of the chief jailer. (v. 21)

What Happened?

It would have been so easy, it would have felt so right, for Joseph to become bitter and revengeful. But he *chose,* instead, to patiently endure prison. And the Lord gave him an inner peace, as well as favor in the eyes of those around him. As before, in Potiphar's house, Joseph's attitude made him a useful tool in God's hands.

> And the chief jailer committed to Joseph's charge
> all the prisoners who were in the jail; so that what-
> ever was done there, he was responsible for it. . . .
> And whatever he did, the Lord made to prosper.
> (vv. 22, 23b)

First and foremost in Joseph's life was his relationship with God. And if God chose to allow him to be put in prison, Joseph saw that as His sovereign right. He didn't argue with God or take it personally. Instead, he recognized that God's hand was in it and approached his new restriction as another opportunity for God to work in his life. Because of that, God was able to use him strategically in the lives of two men.

> Then it came about after these things the cupbearer and the baker for the king of Egypt offended their lord, the king of Egypt. And Pharaoh was furious with his two officials, the chief cupbearer and the chief baker. So he put them in confinement in the house of the captain of the bodyguard, in the jail, the same place where Joseph was imprisoned. And the captain of the bodyguard put Joseph in charge of them, and he took care of them; and they were in confinement for some time. (40:1–4)

We're not told what these men did to offend Pharaoh, but chances are, given their former job titles, it had something to do with Pharaoh's food. The baker obviously prepared his meals and it was the cupbearer's job to taste Pharaoh's food and wine to prevent him from being poisoned.

> Then the cupbearer and the baker for the king of Egypt, who were confined in jail, both had a dream the same night, each man with his own dream and each dream with its own interpretation. When Joseph came to them in the morning and observed them, behold, they were dejected. And he asked Pharaoh's officials who were with him in confinement in his master's house, "Why are your faces so sad today?" (vv. 5–7)

Even though the bottom had dropped out of his life, Joseph's attitude of patient endurance enabled him to be sensitive to the needs of others. And it was this concern for others that started a chain of events that would eventually lead to his release, beginning with the interpretation of the king's servants' dreams.

> Then they said to him, "We have had a dream and there is no one to interpret it." Then Joseph said to them, "Do not interpretations belong to God? Tell it to me, please." (v. 8)

If you'll remember, Joseph had had some experience with dreams before (37:5–11), and all it did was create problems for him. Yet

when he hears that these men are upset because no one can interpret their dreams, he still offers to help.

The First Dream

> So the chief cupbearer told his dream to Joseph,
> and said to him, "In my dream, behold, there was
> a vine in front of me; and on the vine were three
> branches. And as it was budding, its blossoms came
> out, and its clusters produced ripe grapes. Now
> Pharaoh's cup was in my hand; so I took the grapes
> and squeezed them into Pharaoh's cup, and I put the
> cup into Pharaoh's hand." Then Joseph said to him,
> "This is the interpretation of it: the three branches
> are three days; within three more days Pharaoh will
> lift up your head and restore you to your office; and
> you will put Pharaoh's cup into his hand according
> to your former custom when you were his cupbearer."
> (vv. 9–13)

No doubt this was exciting news for the cupbearer. And Joseph
saw the possibility of something good in it for himself too. The next
two verses remind us that Joseph was a real flesh-and-blood human
being, not some pristine saint whose feet never touched the ground.

> "Only keep me in mind when it goes well with you,
> and please do me a kindness by mentioning me to
> Pharaoh, and get me out of this house. For I was in
> fact kidnapped from the land of the Hebrews, and
> even here I have done nothing that they should
> have put me into the dungeon." (vv. 14–15)

The Second Dream

After hearing the cupbearer's good fortune, the baker immediately
launched into his dream. And Joseph faced the unpleasant task of
having to tell him that his wasn't a dream—it was a nightmare.

> When the chief baker saw that he had interpreted
> favorably, he said to Joseph, "I also saw in my dream,
> and behold, there were three baskets of white bread
> on my head; and in the top basket there were some
> of all sorts of baked food for Pharaoh, and the birds
> were eating them out of the basket on my head."

Then Joseph answered and said, "This is its interpretation: the three baskets are three days; within three more days Pharaoh will lift up your head from you and will hang you on a tree; and the birds will eat your flesh off you." (vv. 16–19)

Expectation

Three days later everything happened just as Joseph had said. The cupbearer went back to serving Pharaoh, and the baker became food for the birds (vv. 20–22). While he must have hated to see such a dire interpretation come true, all of this must also have raised some hopeful expectations in Joseph. In his daydreams he could probably see the cupbearer convincing Pharaoh to free him. Mentally, Joseph had his bags packed and was ready to go.

Abandonment: Joseph Forgotten

There was only one problem though. The cupbearer had a short memory.

Yet the chief cupbearer did not remember Joseph,
but forgot him.
Now it happened at the end of two full years
that Pharaoh had a dream. (40:23–41:1a)

There are two important observations we should mention here about Joseph's situation. First, *he was abandoned by a friend.* If an enemy abandons you, who cares? But when it's a friend, that cuts deep. Second, *the abandonment was for a lengthy period of time.* Sometimes we get upset when we're abandoned for even a minute. According to 40:1, Joseph was abandoned for two years.

Earlier, we said there are three different types of mistreatment. But from our study of Joseph's life today we can add another: *Unfair abandonment from one you helped.* All of us can identify with this. Perhaps you've been left by a mate for whom you worked and sacrificed to put through school. Or maybe some of you have started a business with a partner, someone you trusted. And one day somebody hands you the books and you find out this person has been siphoning off the company's profits the whole time you've been in business.

Our natural response to this kind of an experience is to feel disillusioned; first with the person who abandoned us, then with

God. If we allow that feeling to fester long enough, it begins to turn into cynicism and our heart hardens with bitterness.

Disillusionment: Cause and Cure

Disillusionment comes from putting one's complete hope in people. It happens when we put someone on a pedestal and allow that person to take the place of God. This person can be a child, parent, pastor, mate, or friend. They all have feet of clay, and sooner or later that clay will crumble and disappoint you.

There is only one cure for the kind of disillusionment that comes from being mistreated. Put your complete hope and trust in the living Lord. No other vaccine will work!

Joseph would agree with Viktor Frankl—everything can be taken from you except that one precious freedom to choose one's attitude. Joseph chose the cure. And all the mistreatment of his brothers, Potiphar, slavery, or imprisonment could not reduce his hope to the ashes of disillusionment.

 Living Insights

Though destined to have his youthful dreams come true, Joseph's path to their fulfillment was nothing less than nightmarish. He endured every type of mistreatment we could list—undeserved treatment from family members, unexpected restrictions through his circumstances, untrue accusations from people, and finally, unfair abandonment from one he had helped.

How could Pharaoh's cupbearer have so quickly forgotten Joseph? Joseph had interpreted his dream and shown him compassion when the cupbearer was in a painful and frightening situation. Perhaps the painfulness of the cupbearer's situation is the key. To remember Joseph would have meant recalling his time in the dungeon and experiencing all that pain again. So he turned away from it—a tendency we all have—and put the memory out of his mind. Unfortunately, with that memory, Joseph and his request were also thrown out.

- Has there been an experience in your life similar to Joseph's? Has there been a time in your life when someone you helped through a valley of pain turned away and forgot you? Describe the situation.

_____

_____

_____

_____

_____

* Can you crystallize how you felt?

_____

_____

_____

* Did you become disillusioned with this person? Or with God?

_____

_____

_____

* What methods of coping with this abandonment and unfairness have you tried? Have they worked?

_____

_____

_____

 Living Insights   STUDY TWO

Because of the cupbearer's abandonment, Joseph spent two more long years in prison. How did he survive? How did he endure the anguished times of despair and depression that must have come? And how did he come through that excruciating time of injustice with his faith still intact—more than intact, mature and strong?

Perhaps it has something to do with where Joseph ultimately placed his trust.

Do not trust in princes,
In mortal man, in whom there is no salvation.
His spirit departs, he returns to the earth;
In that very day his thoughts perish.
How blessed is he whose help is the God of Jacob,
Whose hope is in the Lord his God; . . .
Who executes justice for the oppressed;
Who gives food to the hungry.
The Lord sets the prisoners free.
(Ps. 146:3–5, 7)

The next time you are feeling forgotten, forsaken, abandoned, and disillusioned, remember that there is One who is unfailingly trustworthy. Here are some Scriptures that will help bring this to mind.

The Trustworthiness of God

Deuteronomy 31:6	Psalm 118:5–9
Psalm 25	Psalm 146
Psalm 27:10	Proverbs 3:5–6
Psalm 37:3–6, 28	Isaiah 42:16
Psalm 94:14	Matthew 28:20b
Psalm 98:3	Hebrews 13:5

Chapter 4

REMEMBERED AND PROMOTED BY GOD

Genesis 41:1–46

Of all the different categories of truth in the Bible, none are more helpful than God's promises—all 7,487 of them.[1] Promises like:

> "Can a woman forget her nursing child,
> And have no compassion on the son of her womb?
> Even these may forget, but I will not forget you.
> Behold, I have inscribed you on the palms of My hands;
> Your walls are continually before Me."
> (Isa. 49:15–16)

> Be anxious for nothing, but in everything by prayer and supplication with thanksgiving let your requests be made known to God. And the peace of God, which surpasses all comprehension, shall guard your hearts and your minds in Christ Jesus. (Phil. 4:6–7)

Of all the promises, though, none are more meaningful than those that promise divine blessing after human suffering, hope after affliction. Let's take a moment to look at some examples of this kind of promise from both the Old and New Testaments.

Promises of Divine Promotion

Tucked away in the Old Testament is a book that reads more like a private journal, a chronicle of calamity. It is named for its main character, Job, and details how he was assaulted by loss, death, dis-

---

1. Herbert Lockyer, *All the Promises of the Bible* (Grand Rapids, Mich.: Zondervan Publishing House, 1962), p. 10. Lockyer records the story of a man named Everet R. Storms who, during his twenty-seventh reading of the Bible, broke down the promises of Scripture as follows: "7,487 promises by God to man, 2 by God the Father to God the Son, 991 by one man to another . . . , 290 by man to God. 21 promises were made by angels, one by man to an angel, and two were made by an evil spirit to the Lord. Satan made nine. . . . Storms then gives us the grand total of 8,810 promises."

ease, grief, and misguided friends. In chapter 23 Job vents some of his frustration over God's seeming silence and hiddenness.

> "Oh that I knew where I might find Him,
> That I might come to His seat!
> I would present my case before Him
> And fill my mouth with arguments. . . .
> Behold, I go forward but He is not there,
> And backward, but I cannot perceive Him;
> When He acts on the left, I cannot behold Him;
> He turns on the right, I cannot see Him."
> (Job 23:3–4, 8–9)

Job wants the *why* and *how long* questions concerning his suffering answered. He wants an opportunity to argue his innocence before God and end his pain and suffering. But he cannot present his case because he cannot find the Judge.

In the midst of this long, dark night of suffering, Job reminds himself of a fact, a promise, a hope.

> "But He knows the way I take;
> When He has tried me, I shall come forth as
> gold." (v. 10)

Notice Job said, "*When* He has tried me," which implies the passage of time. There's no such thing as a quick way to refine gold. The process of refining, purifying, and perfecting gold is a lengthy, painstaking process. In the same way, God uses the painstaking process of our afflictions and sufferings to refine and perfect His goldlike qualities in us.[2]

Over in the New Testament the same kind of promise is anchored amidst some intense affliction in 1 Peter 5. According to verse 6, something was happening that prompted Peter to remind his readers to *humble* themselves and not resist God. Verse 7 addresses feelings of *anxiety*. Verse 8 talks about the enemy, the devil, wanting to *devour* them. And verse 9 plainly states that they were going through some kind of *suffering*, though what it is isn't explicitly stated. Finally, in verse 10 comes the promise that can keep all our lives from being capsized by troubles.

---

2. Keep in mind that all this has nothing to do with externals. Job does not say, "When He has tried me He'll double the wealth he took away," or, "When he has tried me my wife will turn around and say she's sorry, and our relationship will be better than before." No. He's saying "I'll come forth as gold; I'll be wiser, purer, more like Him."

And after you have suffered for a little while, the
God of all grace, who called you to His eternal glory
in Christ, will Himself perfect, confirm, strengthen
and establish you. (v. 10)

When the testing has ended, when the flames have surfaced and
consumed the dross of self-centeredness, you'll come forth as gold.
Don't resist trials and afflictions as intruders. Rather, submit to God
in the midst of them, allowing Him to perfect, confirm, strengthen,
and establish your character for His purposes. A. W. Tozer said,

It is necessary for God to use the hammer, the file
and the furnace in His holy work of preparing a saint
for true sainthood. It is doubtful whether God can
bless a man greatly until He has hurt him deeply.[3]

Joseph had been hurt deeply. God allowed him to be put through
the refining fires of misunderstanding, slavery, false accusations,
imprisonment, abandonment, and more. But there was gold in the
making—a purified character that God could use to greatly bless
the lives of many.

The Test: Darkness before Dawn

In our last study, we saw that Joseph interpreted the cupbearer's
dream, revealing to him that in three days he would be restored to
his former job. In return, Joseph asked that he remember to put in
a good word for him to Pharaoh. But Joseph's new friend promptly
forgot about him for the next two years (41:1). Why would that
sort of thing happen? Because God wasn't through with the gold-
making process. Joseph wasn't quite ready to handle the promotion
that God was preparing for him.

What happened during those two years? Nothing . . . on the
outside. Joseph lived out monotonous, unexciting hours that stacked
up into days, months, and finally years. All that time just waiting
while it seemed like nothing was happening. Humanly speaking,
waiting is one of the most difficult tasks we can be assigned. From
our perspective it feels like we're stagnating and getting nowhere.
But, from God's perspective, it is the ideal crucible for strengthen-
ing and establishing His character in us.

3. A. W. Tozer, *The Root of the Righteous* (Camp Hill, Pa.: Christian Publications, 1986),
p. 137.

The Turning Point: Pharaoh's Dream

Ironically, the turning point in Joseph's life came as a result of another dream.

The Dream Declared

Pharaoh woke up one morning disturbed over two strange dreams. He had first dreamed that there were seven sleek, fat cows who came up out of the Nile and were followed by seven ugly, gaunt cows who devoured them. After this, he dreamed of seven good, plump ears of grain growing on a single stalk, which were then swallowed up by seven thin, scorched ears (vv. 1–7). When Pharaoh awoke, he called for all his magicians and wise men to interpret these dreams for him (v. 8). But none of them could. Suddenly, the cupbearer remembers another interpreter of dreams and immediately begins to pour out a long-forgotten favor.

> Then the chief cupbearer spoke to Pharaoh, saying, "I would make mention today of my own offenses. Pharaoh was furious with his servants, and he put me in confinement in the house of the captain of the bodyguard, both me and the chief baker. And we had a dream on the same night, he and I; each of us dreamed according to the interpretation of his own dream. Now a Hebrew youth was with us there, a servant of the captain of the bodyguard, and we related them to him, and he interpreted our dreams for us. To each one he interpreted according to his own dream. And it came about that just as he interpreted for us, so it happened; he restored me in my office, but he hanged him." (vv. 9–13)

The Dream Interpreted

Pharaoh immediately calls to have Joseph brought up from prison and hurriedly made to shave and change clothes (v. 14).

Just for a moment, put yourself in Joseph's sandals. Why has he been down in that furnace called a dungeon for the past two years? Humanly speaking, it was because the cupbearer forgot him. Now he's suddenly released and standing in front of Pharaoh, the cupbearer's boss. But you won't hear one word of resentment spoken against the cupbearer. Why? Because Joseph kept his eyes on the Lord, not the cupbearer.

And Pharaoh said to Joseph, "I have had a dream, but no one can interpret it; and I have heard it said about you, that when you hear a dream you can interpret it." Joseph then answered Pharaoh, saying, "It is not in me; God will give Pharaoh a favorable answer." (vv. 15–16)

The New International Version says, "I cannot do it." Joseph isn't nitpicking over terms here. He wants it clearly understood that if truth comes, it will come from God and He alone deserves the glory. The years of suffering have purged him and now he has come forth as gold—the kind of gold that refuses even the temptation to use God's gift of interpreting dreams as a bargaining tool to secure his freedom.

Pharaoh then tells Joseph his dreams (vv. 17–24), and Joseph explains that God was telling Pharaoh what He is about to do. The seven sleek, fat cows and the seven plump ears of grain represent seven years of great abundance throughout Egypt. This bumper crop will then be followed by seven years of famine, which in the dream were represented by the gaunt cows and thin grain swallowing up the good. This famine will be so intense that the people will forget there were ever days of plenty (vv. 25–31). Even to the end of the interpretation, Joseph keeps Pharaoh's focus on the Lord and off himself.

"Now as for the repeating of the dream to Pharaoh twice, it means that the matter is determined by God, and God will quickly bring it about." (v. 32)

Pharaoh was powerful, but even the world's greatest army was defenseless against the onslaught of a famine. At this moment of weakness, Joseph provided Pharaoh with the strong counsel he needed to be able to save the Egyptian empire from ruin.

"And now let Pharaoh look for a man discerning and wise, and set him over the land of Egypt. Let Pharaoh take action to appoint overseers in charge of the land, and let him exact a fifth of the produce of the land of Egypt in the seven years of abundance. Then let them gather all the food of these good years that are coming, and store up the grain for food in the cities under Pharaoh's authority, and let them guard it. And let the food become as a reserve for the land for the seven years of famine which will occur in the land of Egypt, so that the land may not perish during the famine." (vv. 33–36)

The Reward: Joseph's Promotion

When Joseph counseled Pharaoh, he spoke directly, honestly, and for God's glory. He wasn't interviewing for a job. But the refined qualities of discernment and wisdom shone through in what he was saying, and they caught Pharaoh's eye.

Honored for His Character

Now the proposal seemed good to Pharaoh and to all his servants. Then Pharaoh said to his servants, "Can we find a man like this, in whom is a divine spirit?" So Pharaoh said to Joseph, "Since God has informed you of all this, there is no one so discerning and wise as you are." (vv. 37–39)

The word *discerning* here means the ability to have shrewd insight into a situation and its needs. And the wisdom Joseph displayed assured Pharaoh that he had this kind of deep perception. So in a stunning reversal, Joseph is given a promotion that will take him in one day from the pit to the pinnacle of Egypt.

Exalted over Egypt

"You shall be over my house, and according to your command all my people shall do homage; only in the throne I will be greater than you." And Pharaoh said to Joseph, "See I have set you over all the land of Egypt." Then Pharaoh took off his signet ring from his hand, and put it on Joseph's hand, and clothed him in garments of fine linen, and put the gold necklace around his neck. And he had him ride in his second chariot; and they proclaimed before him, "Bow the knee!" And he set him over all the land of Egypt. (vv. 40–43)

F. B. Meyer wrote,

It was a wonderful ascent, sheer in a single bound from the dungeon to the steps of the throne. His father had rebuked him; now Pharaoh, the greatest monarch of his time, welcomes him. . . . The hands that were hard with the toils of a slave are adorned with a signet ring. The feet are no longer tormented by fetters; a chain of gold is linked around his neck. The coat of many colours torn from him by violence and defiled by blood, and the garment left in the hand of the adulteress, are exchanged for vestures of fine linen drawn from the royal wardrobe. He was once trampled upon as the offscouring of all things; now all Egypt is commanded to bow before him, as he rides forth in the second chariot, prime minister of Egypt, and second only to the king.[4]

Responses We Can Learn from Joseph

Joseph's Cinderella promotion was incredible. But let's not end our study focusing on the gold necklace he wore and forgetting the gold character underneath it.

That gold character was made possible by two important responses —responses that are not exclusive to Joseph.

First: *During the waiting period, trust God without panic.* We must learn to count on Him to handle the cupbearers of our lives who may forget and abandon us. Second: *During the time of reward, thank God without pride.* Oftentimes the night of our suffering seems as if it will never pass. We feel as if we can't even remember what the dawn was like. In our hearts, we pray for endurance and promise to thank God and give Him the glory when the dawn comes. But that thankfulness, that humility, often vanishes like morning mist when God rewards us. The best way to guard against this is to remember to thank Him—continuously.

 Living Insights STUDY ONE

Though it's clear from Joseph's story that God rewards waiting, it is surely no easy thing for us to do. The crucible of waiting is just that—a place of intense heat, a place where we are melted and molded to the Master's will. Listen to how Ben Patterson describes this process.

4. F. B. Meyer, *Joseph: Beloved—Hated—Exalted* (Fort Washington, Pa.: Christian Literature Crusade, n.d.), p. 62.

Picture a blazing hot forge and a piece of gold thrust into it to be heated until all that is impure and false is burnt out. As it is heated, it is also softened and shaped by the metalworker. Our faith is the gold; our suffering is the fire. The forge is the waiting: it is the tension and longing and, at times, anguish of waiting for God to keep his promises.

It is also the way God makes our character pure and shapes us into the people he wants us to be.[5]

Are you in the crucible of waiting right now? Have you been there long?

_____

What is it that you are waiting for: a job, a mate, a child? Justice, relief, healing? Describe it.

_____

_____

_____

It's true that we must learn to trust God without panic, but just because it's true doesn't mean it's easy. What types of things do you panic over?

_____

_____

_____

Look up the following Scriptures, and write down any insights they give you that might help you turn your panic into trust.

Job 23:10 _____

_____

Isaiah 40:29–31 _____

_____

5. Ben Patterson, *Waiting: Finding Hope When God Seems Silent* (Downers Grove, Ill.: Inter-Varsity Press, 1989), pp. 11–12.

Isaiah 30:18 _____

_____

Jeremiah 29:11 _____

_____

1 Peter 1:6–7 _____

_____

 ### *Living Insights*   STUDY TWO

Sometimes the pain of waiting is beyond earthly words. At those times, only the words of God seem to have any real strength and comfort in them. So if your heart is crying out to God today, if the anguish of your waiting is expressible only through tears, meditate on these words of His and know that He understands.[6]

> Though the fig tree should not blossom,
> And there be no fruit on the vines,
> Though the yield of the olive should fail,
> And the fields produce no food,
> Though the flock should be cut off from the fold,
> And there be no cattle in the stalls,
> Yet I will exult in the Lord,
> I will rejoice in the God of my salvation.
> The Lord God is my strength,
> And He has made my feet like hinds' feet,
> And makes me walk on my high places.
> (Hab. 3:17–19)

> For His anger is but for a moment,
> His favor is for a lifetime;
> Weeping may last for the night,
> But a shout of joy comes in the morning.
> (Ps. 30:5)

---

6. The agony of Gethsemane was Jesus' crucible of waiting—see Luke 22:39–46 and Mark 14:32–41.

Chapter 5

REAPING THE REWARDS
OF RIGHTEOUSNESS
Genesis 41:41–57

On a scale of one to ten, ten being the highest, how positive and affirming are you? Are the private and public conversations you carry on with yourself and others uplifting and supportive? Would you say you're a Mother Teresa nine or a wrecking crew two? One way of finding out is to give yourself the following two tests.

First, think about how encouraging you are when other people are afflicted, depressed, crushed. Do you weep with those who weep?

Second, reflect on how affirming and positive you are when someone who has suffered for a long time is suddenly promoted and becomes prosperous. Isn't it amazing how uncomfortable many of us are with people who are affluent? Even when we have no reason to doubt the source of someone's wealth, we often gravitate toward being critical rather than supportive.

Someone most of us are used to envisioning in difficult circumstances is the apostle Paul. According to 2 Corinthians 11:23–27, he received thirty-nine lashes five times; was beaten with rods three times, stoned once, shipwrecked three times; and was threatened by a host of other dangers on occasions too numerous to mention. But Paul also told the Philippians that not every day of his life was spent enduring some affliction.

> I have learned to be content in whatever circumstances I am. I know how to get along with humble means, and I also know how to live in prosperity; in any and every circumstance I have learned the secret of being filled and going hungry, both of having abundance and suffering need. (Phil. 4:11b–12)

Paul having abundance? Most of us can picture him in pain as a half-starved saint, but a rejoicing well-fed one? No. That's one picture many of us have been conditioned not to see. Why?

The truth is that many of us have been conditioned to think that there's something especially spiritual about the hurting, weeping days of our lives and something very carnal about days of pros-

37

perity. As a result, we tend to be more affirming of those living with humble means and suffering need than we are with those who live in prosperity and have an abundance.

A Brief Review

Today, as we travel back to Joseph's biography in Genesis, let's add to the relevance of our study by imagining Joseph as a contemporary Christian friend. Now, so far, this friend has been through some very difficult days. He was hated and rejected by his own brothers, who sold him to a passing caravan. Later, he was sold again on the slave's auction block in Egypt. Removed from and forgotten by his family, Joseph was forced to learn a new language and culture under the command of Potiphar, the captain of Pharaoh's bodyguard. Meanwhile, Mrs. Potiphar tried repeatedly to seduce Joseph, and when she finally saw that he wouldn't succumb, she falsely accused him of attempted rape. This charge landed him in prison, where he was forgotten by a friend who could possibly have secured his release two years earlier.

Joseph had suffered deeply. And most of us would have rallied around him and given him all the encouragement and support we could. Especially since he continued to walk with God through all this. "I'm praying for you, Joseph." "Don't get discouraged, you did the right thing, Joseph." "Keep trusting in the Lord, Joseph; He hasn't forgotten you!"

In the last seventeen verses of Genesis 41, however, Joseph's life is going to be radically reversed, and we will face the difficult test of success. How supportive will we be when our friend Joseph is suddenly promoted? Let's find out.

A Man Restored

As we saw in our last lesson, Joseph was unexpectedly brought before Pharaoh to interpret two dreams that had troubled the king. In addition, Joseph offered Pharaoh some invaluable counsel that would save the Egyptian empire from ruin. Because of Joseph's discernment and wisdom, Pharaoh immediately promoted him from prisoner to prime minister. And with that promotion came many rewards.

A Position of Great Authority

One by one, Pharaoh bestowed upon Joseph several kinds of authority. First, Joseph received an unlimited territorial authority,

"I have set you over all the land of Egypt" (Gen. 41:41b). The whole land was to be under his control—a land richly nourished by the Nile and covered with cities, stately temples, pyramids, and colossal figures towering over one hundred feet in height.

Pharaoh also gave Joseph carte blanche financial authority, "Then Pharaoh took off his signet ring from his hand, and put it on Joseph's hand" (v. 42a). The term *signet ring* comes from the Hebrew verb that means "to sink down." The ring was used for sinking the Pharaoh's emblem into soft clay. It was like the MasterCard of that day, with all the wealth of Egypt behind it. And now it belonged to Joseph, to make any transaction he deemed necessary.

Joseph also received a whole new wardrobe to match the new royal authority given to him. The prison garments were quickly thrown away and replaced with "garments of fine linen" and a necklace made of gold (v. 42b).

Next, Joseph was given his own company car, Pharaoh's "second chariot," to be driven throughout Egypt to proclaim the new prime minister's public authority.

> And he had him ride in his second chariot; and they proclaimed before him, "Bow the knee!" And he set him over all the land of Egypt. Moreover, Pharaoh said to Joseph, "Though I am Pharaoh, yet without your permission no one shall raise his hand or foot in all the land of Egypt." (vv. 43–44)

Now if Joseph's newly acquired territorial and financial authority didn't bother you, seeing him surrounded by soldiers shouting for everyone to bow the knee and show respect probably does. It's hard to be affirming of that kind of success. We tend to look with a jaundiced eye and ask, "Who does he think he is?"

But the Scriptures never once say that Joseph commanded anyone to bow the knee. In fact, Joseph was probably embarrassed by all the hoopla and overwhelmed by the incredible irony of the situation. For there he was, a Hebrew as Egypt's new prime minister, riding in Pharaoh's chariot with the scars of slavery still on him.

New Name, New Wife

In addition to his new authority, Joseph was also given a new name—Zaphenath-paneah (v. 45a). The small syllable *nath* is a reference to a goddess worshiped in Egypt named Neith. Translated, Pharaoh's new name for Joseph meant "the god speaks and lives."

Certainly this is not the kind of name Joseph would have chosen for himself. But, as Joseph was quickly finding out, there are some things that aren't yours to determine when someone else promotes you to a position of authority.

To promote his social standing in Egypt, Joseph was also given a wife: "Asenath, the daughter of Potiphera priest of On" (v. 45b). Her name, which also includes the syllable *nath,* meant "belonging to Neith." We're not told whether she was bright or dull, attractive or plain, sympathetic to Joseph's faith or antagonistic. Only that she was the daughter of an Egyptian priest.

Youth and a Bright Future

The writer pauses in verse 46 to tell us a significant personal fact about Joseph. This former Hebrew slave who now rules Egypt is only thirty years old.

So often we think God blesses and uses only older men and women in leadership positions. The Bible, however, is filled with examples of young people in leadership positions. Do you know how old David was when Samuel anointed him to be Israel's next king? Not even twenty. When Nebuchadnezzar picked Daniel to serve in his court, he was still in his teens. And Josiah, in 2 Chronicles 34, was only eight years old when he began his reign in Jerusalem.[1]

Joseph was a young man with a very promising future. He had been assured by God that, for the next seven years, Egypt would be blessed with unprecedented bumper crops. And it was.

> Thus Joseph stored up grain in great abundance like
> the sand of the sea, until he stopped measuring it,
> for it was beyond measure. (v. 49)

Now, on a scale of one to ten, would you still be praying for Joseph? Would you still affirm this richly adorned young man who rode in Pharaoh's chariot? Would you still believe in someone who was named "the god speaks and lives" and who was married to the daughter of a pagan priest? To be honest, many of us would probably score only about a one or two on the scale. But we are looking only at the surface. Let's find out what Joseph was like on the inside at this time.

1. There is no lack of evidence outside the Bible, either. Charles Haddon Spurgeon took the pulpit of New Park Street Chapel while still in his teens; before he was thirty, six thousand people were coming each week to the famed London Tabernacle to hear him preach. And another famous preacher, G. Campbell Morgan, was only twelve when he gave his first sermon.

Two Sons and a Clear Conscience

In the next few verses, Joseph uses a play on words that reveals his heart attitude toward God.

> Now before the year of famine came, two sons were born to Joseph, whom Asenath, the daughter of Potiphera priest of On, bore to him. And Joseph named the first-born Manasseh, "For," he said, "God has made me forget all my trouble and all my father's household." And he named the second Ephraim, "For," he said, "God has made me fruitful in the land of my affliction." (vv. 50–52)

The latter part of verse 51 actually reads, God "manassehed" me of all my troubles and all my father's household. What does this mean? The root of the name Manasseh is *nashah*, meaning "to forget." But in the Hebrew construction of this word, Manasseh means "to take the sting out of a memory." Joseph had many painful memories from his troublesome past. But with the birth of his first son, God removed the sting, so Joseph named his firstborn Manasseh.

Ephraim comes from the verb meaning "to be fruitful." The name of this second son was to be a living reminder and testimony that it was God who "ephraimed" Joseph, made him fruitful in the land of his affliction. Underneath the exterior trappings of Egyptian royalty beat a heart that was committed to "bowing the knee" to Jehovah.

Food amidst Famine

The integrity of Joseph's faith and character is also revealed in verses 53–57.

> When the seven years of plenty which had been in the land of Egypt came to an end, and the seven years of famine began to come, just as Joseph had said, then there was famine in all the lands; but in all the land of Egypt there was bread. So when all the land of Egypt was famished, the people cried out to Pharaoh for bread; and Pharaoh said to all the Egyptians, "Go to Joseph; whatever he says to you, you shall do." When the famine was spread over all the face of the earth, then Joseph opened all the storehouses, and sold to the Egyptians; and the famine was severe in the land of Egypt. And the people of

all the earth came to Egypt to buy grain from Joseph,
because the famine was severe in all the earth.

Because Joseph believed God's prediction and was faithful in the execution of his job, Egypt and all the world benefited. Untold thousands survived the famine who otherwise would have perished.

A Word of Hope

On the surface, it wouldn't appear as if many of us have much in common with the Joseph of Genesis 41:41–57. You'll probably never be given the kind of territorial, financial, or public authority he received. It's likely you'll drive to work each day in your own car instead of being picked up by a presidential chariot. No one, not even your best friend, is going to run out in front of you telling people, "Bow the knee!" because you're coming. And what about the clothes Joseph wore? They were designer-royalty linens and gold from Pharaoh's own private haberdashery. And yours?

Don't be too concerned, however, if you don't share all the same exterior trappings as Joseph. The clothes, the chariot—they're all dust anyway. Focus instead on these timeless interior lessons from Joseph's heart.

First: *Lengthy afflictions need not discourage us.* So much of our attention has been focused on what happened to Joseph that many of you may have missed the timing involved. Remember that Joseph was only seventeen when the bottom fell out of his life, and it wasn't until he was thirty that his circumstances significantly improved. Thirteen years of unrelenting affliction! And yet, Joseph didn't allow discouragement to enslave or imprison his heart. How did he do it? The only way possible—he focused on loving God with all his heart, soul, mind, and strength.

Second: *Bad memories need not defeat us.* The past is still present within us in the form of memories. And for many, painful memories are still what's controlling and defeating our attempts to love God and others. But we *can* free ourselves from them. By God's grace, we have the power to choose whom we will serve—a bad memory or a loving God. You may need some help at first, maybe a friend, a close-knit fellowship group, or even a professional counselor. But if you're willing, God can turn that painful wound into a stingless scar.

Third: *Great blessings need not disqualify us.* Often when God promotes a believer, the Christian community tends to be suspicious rather than supportive. Instead, why don't we thank God for the

Josephs He's raising up in our generation? Why don't we get excited about all the ways God is going to use this believer's authority and success in ways we never could? Perhaps if we were more affirming and supportive, there would be fewer who succumb to temptations and fall into ruin.

 ## *Living Insights*

Romans 12:15 tells us to "rejoice with those who rejoice, and weep with those who weep." Our lesson today has highlighted the fact that, for many of us, it's more comfortable to fulfill the latter part of this verse than it is the former. Why do you suppose that is?

Is it because many of us can more readily identify with weeping? Is it because we have an underdog mentality—where we root for the one least likely to win and regard the one in the winner's circle with cool contempt? Or is it because suffering seems somehow more spiritual?

- Why do *you* think it's easier for some to affirm the afflicted than support the successful?

_____

_____

_____

Let's explore this further by personally entering the world of abundance. Imagine for a moment that *you* have become the one who is suddenly successful. After long years of struggling and scraping by, God has handed you a beautifully wrapped package labeled "Prosperity."

- How does this new position in life feel?

_____

_____

_____

- How has this prosperity affected the needs that you have?

  Physical _____

Mental _____

Emotional _____

Spiritual _____

- Are these needs *that* different from when you weren't prosperous?

  _____

  _____

- OK, you can take off those Gucci loafers now and slip back into your Payless specials. Has your imaginary walk in prosperity's shoes helped you understand the need to be more supportive and affirming toward those whom God has blessed?

  _____

- Take a moment to think of some concrete ways to affirm and support a friend or a public figure, such as your pastor. If you are having trouble coming up with ideas, let this simple rule help you get started:

  "And just as you want people to treat you, treat them in the same way." (Luke 6:31)

 ## *Living Insights*

Let's spend some time now exploring the significance of the names Joseph gave his sons.

In our lesson, we saw that Manasseh literally means, "the sting is gone out of the remembrance." Joseph still remembered being stripped and flung into a pit by his brothers, being sold as a slave while they coolly looked on. But the pain of those memories couldn't get at him anymore—God had removed the awful sting.

- Partially buried in the shallows of your mind are probably some stingray-like memories, ready to whip an envenomed spine into your soul when they are disturbed. What are some of these bitter, swollen memories that are painful to the touch?

  _____

_____

_____

_____

_____

_____

- Have you prayed for God to take the sting out of these memories, or are you trying to push them away and forget them yourself—before the poison has been let out?

_____

_____

- From Joseph's experience, we see that God didn't remove the sting three seconds after his "Amen." From your own experience, when did God take the sting out of your painful memories?

_____

- What good was served by His waiting so long to do so?

_____

_____

- Look ahead in Joseph's story to Genesis 45:1–8. What role do you think forgiveness and trust in God's sovereignty have to play in removing the sting from painful memories?

_____

_____

_____

- Have you let trust and forgiveness play their role in removing the sting from the painful memories you listed above?

_____

_____

Genesis 41:52 tells us that Joseph named his second son Ephraim, "'For,' he said, 'God has made me fruitful in the land of my affliction.'" We've seen how God made Joseph prosper materially. Now let's take a look at the spiritual fruit.

• What were some of the spiritual fruits God cultivated in Joseph's life (compare Gal. 5:22–23)?

_____

_____

_____

_____

_____

_____

_____

• In your times of affliction, how has God made you fruitful?

_____

_____

_____

_____

_____

_____

_____

Why don't you pause right now and thank God for the hope He has given you—that your land of affliction doesn't have to be a barren and desolate place, but by His grace, it can bloom with tender fruit and fragrant blossoms.

Chapter 6

ACTIVATING A SEARED CONSCIENCE

Genesis 42:1–28

Once upon a time there lived a king and queen who wept every day because they had no children. One day, however, the queen received a prophecy that within a year she would have a child. A year passed, and happily, the prophecy came true. Immediately, a great celebration was planned in honor of the favored child. The guests included friends, relatives, and twelve kind, wise women who could endow the child with fairy gifts.

On the day of the great feast, however, the celebrations were interrupted by the sudden appearance of an uninvited guest—a thirteenth wise woman, a very sinister fairy. In a jealous rage over not being invited, she cast an evil spell on the royal couple's daughter, prophesying that on her fifteenth birthday she would prick her finger with a spindle and die. When the foul intruder left, there was one wise woman who had not yet bestowed her fairy gift. Though she could not undo the wicked decree, she could soften it. Instead of dying, the king's daughter would fall into an enchanted sleep.

The king didn't want to take any chances, however, and commanded that all the spindles in the kingdom be burned. But despite all his efforts, his beautiful daughter pricked her finger with a spindle on her fifteenth birthday and slept for a hundred years. On the very day that the hundred years ended, a prince found his way into the castle, wandered into the room where the beautiful princess lay sleeping, woke her with a kiss, and they lived happily ever after.

Recognize the story? If you guessed *Sleeping Beauty,* you're right —partly. This Brothers Grimm tale also closely parallels the real events in Joseph's story.

Remember how Jacob and Rachel, Joseph's father and mother, had lamented a long time before having their firstborn, Joseph. And how, like the daughter, Joseph was also a favored and gifted child. But because of his brothers' jealous anger, he too was threatened with death. This great evil was "softened," however, by the oldest brother who intervened on Joseph's behalf. Instead of being cast into a deep sleep at fifteen as the princess was, Joseph was cast into a pit when he was seventeen. And, as we have already seen, it was the Prince of Peace who rescued Joseph by enabling him to patiently endure his sufferings and by later promoting him to prince of Egypt.

But everything is not yet "happily ever after" in Joseph's life. In an ironic twist, the prince of Egypt is about to come to the rescue of the very brothers who rejected him. In his commentary on Joseph, F. B. Meyer describes what has happened to the brothers since they sold Joseph so many years ago.

> Meanwhile, the sons had become middle-aged men, with families of their own. They probably never mentioned that deed of violence to each other. *They did their best to banish the thought from their minds.* Sometimes in their dreams they may have caught a glimpse of that young face in its agony, or heard the beseechings of his anguished soul; but they sought to drown such painful memories by deep draughts of the Lethe-stream[1] of forgetfulness. Conscience slept.[2]

For approximately twenty-five years conscience has slept. But, as we shall see in our study today, Joseph's brothers are about to meet the prince whom God will use to wake their slumbering consciences and reunite a divided house.

Famine in Canaan

For the past several chapters and years in Joseph's biography, our focus has been on Joseph's plight in Egypt. And in the latter part of Genesis 41 we were told that the severe famine which struck Egypt also spread "over all the face of the earth." Now, beginning in Genesis 42, our focus suddenly shifts from the well-stocked granaries of Egypt to the empty cupboards of Canaan, from Joseph to Joseph's father and brothers.

> Now Jacob saw that there was grain in Egypt,
> and Jacob said to his sons, "Why are you staring at

---

1. "A river in Hades whose waters cause drinkers to forget their past." *Webster's Ninth New Collegiate Dictionary,* see "lethe."

2. F. B. Meyer, *Joseph: Beloved—Hated—Exalted* (Fort Washington, Pa.: Christian Literature Crusade, n.d.), p. 69.

one another?" And he said, "Behold, I have heard that there is grain in Egypt; go down there and buy some for us from that place, so that we may live and not die." Then ten brothers of Joseph went down to buy grain from Egypt. But Jacob did not send Joseph's brother Benjamin with his brothers, for he said, "I am afraid that harm may befall him." So the sons of Israel came to buy grain among those who were coming, for the famine was in the land of Canaan also. (vv. 1–5)

As we follow the brothers on their journey to Egypt, remember that none of them had any idea where Joseph had ended up or even if he was still alive. Nor did Joseph know anything about what had become of his family or that he was about to encounter his brothers in Egypt.

Encounter in Egypt

Egypt became the soup kitchen for a starving world. Each week thousands came to buy food from the wise prime minister who had faithfully prepared for the wintry seven-year famine.

Dialogue with Joseph

When Jacob's sons finally did reach Egypt, they stood in line with the rest of the gaunt-faced foreigners to buy grain.

Now Joseph was the ruler over the land; he was the one who sold to all the people of the land. And Joseph's brothers came and bowed down to him with their faces to the ground. When Joseph saw his brothers he recognized them, but he disguised himself to them and spoke to them harshly. And he said to them, "Where have you come from?" And they said, "From the land of Canaan, to buy food."

But Joseph had recognized his brothers, although they did not recognize him. (vv. 6–8)

There's a play on words here in the Hebrew. Using the same root word with different verb stems it says, in verse 7, that Joseph recognized his brothers but he made himself unrecognizable.

To help us gain a deeper appreciation of this scene, let's look at some of the reasons why it would've been difficult for Joseph's brothers to recognize him.

First, remember that more than twenty years have passed. The teenager the brothers had known was now a mature man in his forties. Joseph's voice has matured, and he is also fluently speaking a foreign language as if it were his native tongue. Also, the Joseph they had known could speak Hebrew, but this individual uses an interpreter to carry on their conversation (v. 23). They also didn't recognize him because Hebrews wear beards, and Joseph's face is clean-shaven in the manner of the Egyptians. Everything Joseph is wearing, from his headdress on down, has an Egyptian designer label, not Jewish. And even if the brothers had anticipated the remote possibility of seeing Joseph, they would have been searching the faces of Hebrew slaves, not Egyptian royalty. On top of all this, Joseph disguised his kinship even further by speaking harshly to them.

But Joseph immediately recognized his brothers, and certain dreams he'd had long ago began replaying in his mind when he saw them bowing before him (v. 9a). He had dreamed that his brother's harvested sheaves bowed down before him, and here they were, all except the youngest, Benjamin. And he had also dreamed that the sun, moon, and twelve stars—Joseph's whole family—bowed down before him. Finally, the puzzling pieces of his youthful dreams were coming together (37:6–7, 9).

But they were bowing down and showing respect to the prime minister of Egypt, not their brother Joseph. Somehow he had to find out, without revealing who he was, whether they still hated him, whether they had since felt any sorrow or guilt over what they had done to him. One commentator said, "When the test of severe trouble is applied, and when men are thrown out of all conventional modes of thinking and speaking," that is when the true character of the heart is revealed.[3] And this is exactly the kind of test we see Joseph apply to his brothers.

Plan of Joseph

> "You are spies; you have come to look at the unde-
> fended parts of our land." Then they said to him,
> "No, my lord, but your servants have come to buy
> food. We are all sons of one man; we are honest

---

3. Marcus Dods, as quoted by H. C. Leupold in *Exposition of Genesis* (Grand Rapids, Mich.: Baker Book House, 1942), vol. 2, p. 1048.

men, your servants are not spies." Yet he said to them, "No, but you have come to look at the undefended parts of our land!" But they said, "Your servants are twelve brothers in all, the sons of one man in the land of Canaan; and behold, the youngest is with our father today, and one is no more." (42:9b–13)

"One is no more"? *But what if he isn't? Joseph thought. What if he's alive and standing here in front of you? Will you rejoice and embrace him, or remain bedfellows with your seared consciences?* So Joseph applies even more pressure.

And Joseph said to them, "It is as I said to you, you are spies; by this you will be tested: by the life of Pharaoh, you shall not go from this place unless your youngest brother comes here!" (vv. 14–15)

"In all this," F. B. Meyer comments,

I believe *he repeated exactly the scene at the pit's mouth;* and indeed we may perhaps see what really happened there [twenty years before], reflected in the mirror of this scene. It is not unlikely that when they saw him coming towards them, in his princelike dress, they had rushed at him, accusing him of having come to spy out their corrupt behaviour, and take back an evil report to their father, as he had done before: if so, this will explain why he now suddenly accused them of being spies. No doubt the lad protested that he was no spy—that he had only come to inquire after their welfare; but they had met his protestations with rude violence in much the same way as the rough-speaking governor now treated them. . . . If this were the case—and it seems most credible—it is obvious that it was a powerful appeal to their conscience and memory, and one that could not fail to awaken both.[4]

Then, without warning, Joseph decided to imprison them all (v. 17). Why? Probably to give them time to reflect, time to awaken

---

4. Meyer, *Joseph*, p. 72.

their consciences to the way they had sinned against the brother who was "no more," and time for himself to carefully plan his next move. At the end of three days, Joseph altered his original plan. Instead of keeping all of them except one, he decided to keep one and release the others to go and bring the youngest brother back (vv. 18–20).

At this moment the brothers began speaking in Hebrew, thinking that Pharaoh's prime minister wouldn't understand any of it. But Joseph did understand (v. 23).

> Then they said to one another, "Truly we are guilty concerning our brother, because we saw the distress of his soul when he pleaded with us, yet we would not listen; therefore this distress has come upon us." And Reuben answered them, saying, "Did I not tell you, 'Do not sin against the boy'; and you would not listen? Now comes the reckoning for his blood." (vv. 21–22)

To fully appreciate the intensity of this conversation, it's helpful to know that the word *we* used here in the Hebrew is extremely emphatic. "*We* are guilty"; "*we* saw the distress of his soul"; "*we* would not listen." In his *Exposition of Genesis*, H. C. Leupold notes,

> Whatever they may have said in prison, now at least they speak in terms of their guilt in the matter of Joseph. Their conscience has awakened mightily during these three days. They feel that a just retribution has come upon them, and are apparently all of one mind in regard to the matter. They admit guilt, the "only acknowledgment of sin in the book of Genesis."[5]

One of the first signs of a conscience wakening is the admission of personal guilt. Notice that the brothers didn't blame their father for being passive; they didn't blame Joseph for being proud in his mid-teen years; they simply confessed their own guilt.

The brothers also talked about a *transfer of distress* (v. 21). The distress that Joseph had felt in his soul the day they sold him had now entered their own souls via ten fully roused consciences.

---

5. H. C. Leupold, *Exposition of Genesis*, vol. 2, p. 1053.

How did all these emotions and words affect Joseph? The prime minister left the room—so he could weep tears of relief and joy (v. 24a). For years he had waited, hoping he could be reconciled to his brothers and be part of his family again. Now that day was dawning.

When he regained his composure, Joseph had Simeon bound (v. 24b) and ordered the provisions for his brothers' trip home (v. 25). What his brothers didn't know is that he had given them back all the money they paid for the grain they were carrying. Once they discovered the money, it says they "turned trembling to one another, saying, 'What is this that God has done to us?'" (v. 28). Not only have their awakened consciences led them to admit their guilt, now they're beginning to sense God's hand in their strange events.

God in Circumstances

"Once upon a time . . ." Perhaps no other four words, in any language, carry such power to awaken our slumbering imaginations for a Peter Pan flight from reality to fantasy. Today, however, we have flown from fantasy to reality to help us see and remember how God used the prince of Egypt to awaken the sleeping consciences of his brothers.

Before we leave Joseph's world to reenter our own, here are two important lessons to remember. First, *God activates our seared consciences when we are victims of unfair treatment similar to what we once gave someone else.* God used the distress of being falsely accused and imprisoned to rouse the brothers' consciences, bringing to mind the distress they had caused Joseph.

Second, *God activates our seared consciences when we are recipients of undeserved expressions of grace.* His brothers deserved imprisonment or even worse for what they had done to Joseph. But what they received instead was their money back for the grain they were carrying home to Canaan. It was an act of grace from Joseph that God used to further convict his brothers and draw their attention toward Him.

 Living Insights

Every day Joseph's ten older brothers had to choose whether to continue living a lie or to break free of their self-imposed darkness and walk in the light of truth. And every day of those twenty-plus years they had chosen to lie. Bit by bit, they had seared their consciences, until they were so mentally impotent that all they could do at the threshold of a life-or-death situation was stand "staring at one another" (Gen. 42:1).

Have you ever stood where Joseph's brothers did, trapped in a pit of denial that robbed you of the ability to think and to be truly alive?

_____

Did you experience a transfer of distress—the same anguish you once caused another?

_____

_____

How does this idea of a transfer of distress tie in with Galatians 6:7?

_____

_____

_____

_____

In the future, how could you prevent a transfer of distress and experience a transfer of grace instead (see Eph. 4:31–32, 1 Cor. 13:4–7)?

_____

_____

 Living Insights STUDY TWO

Let's use today's study to meditate on some wise words from C. S. Lewis. As you are reading, take time to search your heart and conscience for any places that might be seared. If you find any such areas, bring them before God, for as the psalmist said, "A broken and a contrite heart, O God, Thou wilt not despise" (Ps. 51:17b).

Every time you make a choice you are turning the central part of you, the part of you that chooses, into something a little different from what it was before. And taking your life as a whole, with all your innumerable choices, all your life long you are slowly turning this central thing either into a heavenly creature or into a hellish creature: either into a creature that is in harmony with God, and with other creatures, and with itself, or else into one that is in a state of war and hatred with God, and with its fellow-creatures, and with itself. To be the one kind of creature is . . . joy and peace and knowledge and power. To be the other means madness, horror, idiocy, rage, impotence, and eternal loneliness. Each of us at each moment is progressing to the one state or the other.

That explains what always used to puzzle me about Christian writers; they seem to be so very strict at one moment and so very free and easy at another. They talk about mere sins of thought as if they were immensely important: and then they talk about the most frightful murders and treacheries as if you had only got to repent and all would be forgiven. But I have come to see that they are right. What they are always thinking of is the mark which the action leaves on that tiny central self which no one sees in this life but which each of us will have to endure—or enjoy—for ever. One man may be so placed that his anger sheds the blood of thousands, and another so placed that however angry he gets he will only be laughed at. But the little mark on the soul may be much the same in both. Each has done something to himself which, unless he repents, will make it harder for him to keep out of the rage next time he is tempted, and will make the rage worse when he does fall into it. Each of them, if he seriously turns to God, can have that twist in the central man straightened out again: each is, in the long run, doomed if he will not.[6]

6. C. S. Lewis, *Mere Christianity*, rev. and enl. (New York, N.Y.: Macmillan Publishing Co., Collier Books, 1952), pp. 72–73.

Chapter 7

GROANINGS OF A SAD DAD
Genesis 42:29–43:15

Have you ever accidentally dropped a peanut butter and jelly sandwich? In that split second before impact, your eyes widen with childlike optimism and horror. You hope you're about to witness the miracle of the world's first peanut butter and jelly sandwich landing right side up. But you're also horrified by the possibilities if the sandwich belly flops. Who knows, though, maybe this time will be different, maybe despite gravity and Murphy's Law, your little sandwich will be the sandwich that could, maybe, oh just maybe . . . *splat!* Sigh.

What's worse is when we have days where everything we do seems to land peanut butter and jelly side down. Days when there seems to be this inexorable force thwarting and frustrating our every move. Days like Alexander's terrible, horrible, no good, very bad day.

> I went to sleep with gum in my mouth and now there's gum in my hair and when I got out of bed this morning I tripped on the skateboard and by mistake I dropped my sweater in the sink while the water was running and I could tell it was going to be a terrible, horrible, no good, very bad day.[1]

Natural Tendencies in All of Us

All of us have days like Alexander's. And early on we develop three reflexive responses to the "no good, very bad days" of our lives, responses that are deeply rooted in our human nature.

First, we all tend to respond negatively when things don't go the way we planned. When a business deal falls through, when the car won't start, or when a misunderstanding severs a relationship, our immediate response is typically negative instead of positive.

Second, we all tend to view problems horizontally, from a strictly human point of view, rather than from a vertical, godly perspective.

---

1. Judith Viorst, *Alexander and the Terrible, Horrible, No Good, Very Bad Day* (New York, N.Y.: Atheneum, 1972).

Usually, it's only after we've made things worse by trying to solve a problem on our own that we begin to look at things from His perspective.

Third, we all tend to resist rather than tolerate new ideas— especially if they seem to offer something for nothing! "Nothing's free in this world," we're told, so we condition ourselves to be suspicious and closed toward anything unexpected that doesn't carry a price tag in plain view.

If not dealt with, all three of these natural tendencies will grow stronger as we grow older. Joseph's father, Jacob, could testify to that. Even though he had known God for well over a hundred years, Jacob's faith was constantly being undermined by his negativism, horizontal viewpoint, and closed-mindedness.

Jacob's Initial Resistance and Reluctance

Beginning in Genesis 42:29, the narrative focus of Joseph's biography transports us to Canaan at the time Jacob's ten sons are returning from buying grain in Egypt. Instead of this being a happy occasion, however, it's about to become a terrible, horrible, no good, very bad day for Jacob.

The Return and the Report

To help you see things from Jacob's perspective, imagine you're hearing his sons' story for the first time, just as he is.

> When they came to their father Jacob in the land of Canaan, they told him all that had happened to them, saying, "The man, the lord of the land, spoke harshly with us, and took us for spies of the country. But we said to him, 'We are honest men; we are not spies. We are twelve brothers, sons of our father; one is no more, and the youngest is with our father today in the land of Canaan.' And the man, the lord of the land, said to us, 'By this I shall know that you are honest men: leave one of your brothers with me and take grain for the famine of your households, and go. But bring your youngest brother to me that I may know that you are not spies, but honest men. I will give your brother to you, and you may trade in the land.'" (vv. 29–34)

Did you notice the two important details the sons left out about their trip? They avoided mentioning the three days they spent in prison (42:17), and nothing was said about the money they discovered in one of their grain sacks on the trip home (v. 27).

We don't know exactly what Jacob is thinking while he listens to his sons' incredible tale. But remember, his entire background has been filled with deceit and manipulation, so it's deeply ingrained in his nature to think the worst. And it wasn't long before things did go from bad to worse, and Jacob's natural tendencies began to show.

Discovery and Discussion

> Now it came about as they were emptying their sacks, that behold, every man's bundle of money was in his sack; and when they and their father saw their bundles of money, they were dismayed. (v. 35)

Here they are in the midst of a desperate famine with no crops and no way to earn a living from the soil, and they find all this money. But their reaction isn't, "Praise God, He has provided," or, "Thank the Lord for prompting that prince in Egypt to be generous toward us." Instead, it says they were "dismayed," which in Hebrew means "they were afraid."[2]

Immediately, Jacob's fear flips open the lid on his Pandora's box of natural tendencies, and his negativism, horizontal viewpoint, and resistant attitude come pouring out.

> And their father Jacob said to them, "You have bereaved me of my children: Joseph is no more, and Simeon is no more, and you would take Benjamin; all these things are against me." (v. 36)

"All these things are against me." Sounds pretty paranoid, doesn't it? In all of this Jacob never once stops to think or ask what God might be doing. The oldest son, Reuben, senses that his father's mind is quickly closing and becoming resistant to letting Benjamin go, so he makes a last-ditch offer.

> Then Reuben spoke to his father, saying, "You may put my two sons to death if I do not bring him back

---

2. This is the same word Adam used to describe his feelings toward God after he had sinned, "I heard the sound of Thee in the garden, and I was afraid . . ." (Gen. 3:10a).

to you; put him in my care, and I will return him to you." But Jacob said, "My son shall not go down with you; for his brother is dead, and he alone is left. If harm should befall him on the journey you are taking, then you will bring my gray hair down to Sheol in sorrow." (vv. 37–38)

But Reuben is too late. Jacob is emphatic and the door is shut—for a while.

Jacob's Final Acceptance

As our study continues into the next chapter of Genesis, we're going to see Jacob go through a progression of four phases in his struggle to deal with his circumstances.

Denial and Delay

Now the famine was severe in the land. So it came about when they had finished eating the grain which they had brought from Egypt, that their father said to them, "Go back, buy us a little food." Judah spoke to him, however, saying, "The man solemnly warned us, 'You shall not see my face unless your brother is with you.' If you send our brother with us, we will go down and buy you food. But if you do not send him, we will not go down; for the man said to us, 'You shall not see my face unless your brother is with you.'" (vv. 1–5)

The denial phase is firmly rooted in Jacob's words, "My son shall *not* go down with you" (42:38a, emphasis added). Jacob refuses to admit the necessity of Benjamin's leaving. He won't even look at it or discuss it with his other sons. Then he couples his denial with a delay. Jacob eats the grain and attempts to go about business as usual, in hopes that the problem will go away. But the famine persists and it forces him, again, to face the sensitive topic of Egypt. But even when Jacob does address the need for food, he still completely ignores the real problem: they cannot return for more grain without Benjamin. Judah's reminder, however, moves his father into a second phase.

Blame and Deceit

Then Israel said, "Why did you treat me so badly by telling the man whether you still had another brother?"

59

But they said, "The man questioned particularly about us and our relatives, saying, 'Is your father still alive? Have you another brother?' So we answered his questions. Could we possibly know that he would say, 'Bring your brother down'?" And Judah said to his father Israel, "Send the lad with me, and we will arise and go, that we may live and not die, we as well as you and our little ones. I myself will be surety for him; you may hold me responsible for him. If I do not bring him back to you and set him before you, then let me bear the blame before you forever. For if we had not delayed, surely by now we could have returned twice." (vv. 6–10)

Instead of dealing with the real issues, Jacob digresses into blaming his sons for all his troubles. He also clearly suggests, true to his character, that it would have been better if they had deceived the Egyptian official. Again Judah speaks, this time offering a solution to the problem, and Jacob's resolve against the inevitable begins to weaken.

Tolerance and Uncertainty

Then their father Israel said to them, "If it must be so, then do this: take some of the best products of the land in your bags, and carry down to the man as a present, a little balm and a little honey, aromatic gum and myrrh, pistachio nuts and almonds. And take double the money in your hand, and take back in your hand the money that was returned in the mouth of your sacks; perhaps it was a mistake." (vv. 11–12)

Grim-faced, Jacob agrees to let Benjamin go, but not without gifts and money to assuage the suspicion of the Egyptian official. This same ploy had worked for Jacob once before when he took presents to his brother Esau whom he had cheated (see 32:3–33:11). It's the best horizontal plan Jacob can think of to help ensure Benjamin's safety. Up till now, there are no vertical plans of hoping and trusting in the Lord, only a feeble hope in the horizontal, "perhaps it was a mistake."

Guarded Faith and Abandonment

"Take your brother also, and arise, return to the man; and may God Almighty grant you compassion in the sight of the man, that he may release to you your other brother and Benjamin. And as for me, if I am bereaved of my children, I am bereaved." So the men took this present, and they took double the money in their hand, and Benjamin; then they arose and went down to Egypt and stood before Joseph. (vv. 13–15)

Finally, in this last phase, Jacob at least offers a prayer. Perfunctory though it may be, the words still show a glimmer of faith. A glimmer that is quickly obscured, however, by Jacob's stoic resignation, "If I am bereaved of my children, I am bereaved." This is not awe-inspiring faith.

But haven't we all had terrible, horrible, no good, very bad days like his? Days where our faith lost its struggle against the undercurrents of negativism, a horizontal viewpoint, and resistance to new ideas? Let's not be too hard on Jacob just because we've seen him warts and all today. Rather, let's focus on three techniques for helping ourselves learn to swim against the tide of our natural tendencies.

Practical Techniques for All of Us

First: *Realize and admit your negative mentality.* Confession is the first part of the cure. This may sound elementary, but you'd be surprised at how many Christians have never learned or put into practice this fundamental truth. There's no skipping this elementary principle, no matter how smart you are, if you ever plan to major in a godly mentality.

Second: *Force a vertical focus until it begins to flow freely.* Our natural tendencies have a running start on all of us. From the moment we were born they have been active, growing, and maturing right alongside our physical bodies. By the time we realize these problems and decide to do something about them, we're up against formidable enemies. That's why we must force a vertical focus until it begins to flow freely.

The tendency to view life horizontally is not going to lie down and surrender just because we want it to. It has to be aggressively rooted out and replaced time and again with a vertical perspective. How? One way is to get into the habit of asking yourself questions such as, "Could God be in this?" or "How would the Lord react to this?" or "Do the Scriptures specifically address what my attitude or action should be in this circumstance?"

Third: *Stay open to a new idea for at least five minutes.* Try holding off five minutes before you decide whether to accept or reject a new thought or development. Because once you've made a hasty decision, your pride will do everything it can to keep you from backing down.

None of us can escape having terrible, horrible, no good, very bad days in a fallen world. And it's not just what happens to us that makes life hard, it's also our *response* to those problems and surprises we encounter that often makes life even harder. Are your responses making your life harder?

 Living Insights

Like his son Joseph, Jacob was a man well acquainted with pain and grief. But what a difference in the way the two men faced the hardships life brought them! Where Joseph responded to unfair treatment with integrity and trust in God, Jacob had only his own checkered character and a timid, fearful faith in God to fall back on.

But before we go pointing our finger at Jacob, most of us would probably have to admit that we, too, respond to life's difficulties more like Jacob than like Joseph. So let's use our time today to examine our own responses and identify any trouble spots.

Take the three natural responses we noted in our lesson—reacting negatively, viewing problems horizontally, and resisting new ideas —and prioritize them, listing first the one you struggle with most.

1. _____

2. _____

3. _____

Can you think of a recent example where one of these responses has made your life harder? Explain how.

_____

_____

_____

_____

_____

_____

Let's turn to Study Two to find a way to change these responses and make your life a little easier.

 Living Insights

In our last study we identified our responses. Now let's explore how we can change them, utilizing the three practical techniques with which we closed our lesson.

- *Realize and admit your negative mentality.* Our lesson taught us that the key to victory in this area is confession. As Christians we naturally—and rightly—think that this means bringing our attitudes and responses before God. This is the first step toward change. But it's also important to take the second step, which is enlisting the help of a trusted friend (compare James 5:16 with Gal. 6:2). Is there someone in your life with whom you feel safe enough to admit your negative tendencies? Write down that person's name.

_____

Make an appointment with this person within the next week, and talk as openly and honestly as you can.

- *Force a vertical focus until it begins to flow freely.* Sometimes in the midst of a trial it's so easy to forget that God is still there, isn't it? But we aren't, as the old song goes, "lost in the stars"; God is here, and He isn't leaving. What are some concrete things you can start doing today to retrain your mind to see Him in everything around you, including painful situations?

_____

_____

_____

_____

- *Stay open to a new idea for at least five minutes.* In the space provided, make a list of areas you typically approach with a closed mind. For example, maybe you are resistant to new ideas from your children, an employee, your spouse, or maybe even from your own creative self. Whatever they may be, list these areas so that you know what you are dealing with.

_____

_____

_____

_____

_____

Now, for at least the next two days, consciously try to allow new ideas at least five minutes' time to come to life. You may be surprised at how creative you and those around you really are!

Chapter 8

AT LAST, TOGETHER
...ALMOST

Genesis 43:15-34

In a 1973 article, "Home at Last!" *Newsweek* magazine wonderfully captured the elation in the homecoming of the first few POWs from Vietnam.

> Everything was meticulously planned. The plane would land, the waiting brass would snap to attention, the men would disembark and proceed through an orderly reception line. But when Air Force Maj. Arthur Burer and four other returning POW's arrived at Andrews Air Force Base, it didn't quite work out that way. At the first sight of her husband, Nancy Burer shrieked with happiness and—with her children in hot pursuit—streaked across the tarmac. She leapt into his waiting arms, and he lifted her up in a bear-hug embrace and gleefully whirled her around and around.[1]

Few scenes in life are more emotional than a family reunited after long years of separation. Their eyes are wet, their noses are running, they're shouting and dancing, they're hugging, kissing, touching one another—they're a family again.

It's this kind of emotion that underlies our study today. It has been well over twenty years since Joseph was separated from his family. And now, finally, there's to be a reunion. All of Joseph's brothers, including his full brother, Benjamin, are coming to Egypt, they're going to be a family again—almost.[2]

---

1. "Home at Last!" *Newsweek*, February 26, 1973, p. 16.

2. What we're about to see from Joseph's perspective is a long-awaited reunion. And yet not a complete family reunion, for Joseph's father is still back in Canaan, and his brothers still aren't aware that the Egyptian prime minister is Joseph. From the brothers' perspective, the only reunion they're anticipating is the one with their brother Simeon, who was held captive in Egypt until they returned.

En Route from Canaan to Egypt

As we saw in our last lesson, Joseph's brothers returned to Canaan with the disconcerting news that Simeon had been left bound in Egypt and that they couldn't return for him or more grain without their youngest brother, Benjamin. Jacob flatly refused, however, to send Benjamin. He had already lost Benjamin's mother, Rachel, and their favored firstborn, Joseph. He wasn't about to risk losing their only other son. But when the grain they brought from Egypt was depleted, Jacob relented and Benjamin is allowed to go with his brothers to buy more.

In addition to Benjamin, the brothers also take with them the best products from the land of Canaan as a present and double the amount of money they had found in their grain sacks when they returned from Egypt (Gen. 43:15).

But besides the money, the present, and Benjamin, the brothers also carry back to Egypt a guilty conscience over what they had done to Joseph. Added to that guilt are also feelings of apprehension and uncertainty about the intentions of the suspicious Egyptian prime minister. Will he release Simeon? Will he let them return? Or will he use the money they found in their sacks as an excuse to imprison them?

Fearful Brothers with Joseph's Butler

Our story quickly shifts from the worried and guilt-ridden brothers to the calm and rested brother, Joseph, who has been patiently waiting for their return.

Banquet Plans

> When Joseph saw Benjamin with them, he said
> to his house steward, "Bring the men into the house,
> and slay an animal and make ready; for the men are
> to dine with me at noon." (v. 16)

The wording of this verse indicates that Joseph is primarily interested in seeing Benjamin. Why? Because Benjamin was Joseph's only full brother in the family. And perhaps because Benjamin was just a child when Joseph last saw him more than twenty years ago. Seeing his younger brother now is like seeing him for the first time all over again. Implied in those four simple words, "When Joseph saw Benjamin," is an emotional reunion that almost defies description.

Not only is Joseph immensely relieved to finally behold Benjamin, he is also, in that same moment, reassured that his brothers spoke the truth to him on their first trip.

Uneasy Explanation

Shakespeare once wrote, "Suspicion always haunts the guilty mind."[3] So when Joseph's steward escorted the brothers to the prime minister's home instead of the public grain mart, the guilt-ridden brothers immediately became suspicious.

> Now the men were afraid, because they were brought to Joseph's house; and they said, "It is because of the money that was returned in our sacks the first time that we are being brought in, that he may seek occasion against us and fall upon us, and take us for slaves with our donkeys." (v. 18)

Hounded by insecurities, Joseph's brothers feel the need to assuage their guilt by explaining themselves, by setting the record straight. Even if it means telling everything to a perfect stranger who can do nothing about it.

> So they came near to Joseph's house steward, and spoke to him at the entrance of the house, and said, "Oh, my lord, we indeed came down the first time to buy food, and it came about when we came to the lodging place, that we opened our sacks, and behold, each man's money was in the mouth of his sack, our money in full. So we have brought it back in our hand. We have also brought down other money in our hand to buy food; we do not know who put our money in our sacks." (vv. 19–22)

Calming Response

The brothers, uneasy and afraid, fear the worst and look at the situation from a totally horizontal perspective . . . just like their father. Interestingly, it's the Egyptian steward who speaks of their God and makes them aware of His provision.

---

3. Quoted in *Bartlett's Familiar Quotations*, 15th ed., rev. and enl., ed. Emily Morison Beck (Boston, Mass.: Little, Brown and Co., 1980), p. 186.

And he said, "Be at ease, do not be afraid. Your God
and the God of your father has given you treasure
in your sacks; I had your money." (v. 23a)

To help calm the brothers, the steward not only offers them
encouragement, he communicates it in Hebrew, the brothers' own
language. He says, "Shalom to you," *be at ease,* and, "Elohim," *your
God,* the God of your father has given you treasure. It's the first
time anyone has suggested seeing the money they found in their
sacks from a divine perspective.

The brothers have barely finished hearing the steward's astonish-
ing words when they are hit with a second unexpected surprise.
"Then he brought Simeon out to them" (v. 23b). Now they are
really confused. Here they are, standing at the entrance of the
prime minister's home, whom they haven't even seen yet, and
already their brother is being released to them. What can possibly
happen next? Well,

then the man brought the men into Joseph's house
and gave them water, and they washed their feet;
and he gave their donkeys fodder. (v. 24)

Grateful Brothers with Joseph

Can you imagine how bewildered the brothers must have felt?
They came fearing the worst and, so far, have been given only the
best. Still, the brothers cannot imagine the harsh prime minister
being gracious to them, so they prepare to present their gift in the
hope that it will appease his anger (v. 25).

Reunion

Finally, Joseph comes home. And unbeknownst to the eleven,
the brother who was rejected years ago is about to bring his family
another step closer to being reunited.

When Joseph came home, they brought into the
house to him the present which was in their hand
and bowed to the ground before him. Then he asked
them about their welfare, and said, "Is your old father
well, of whom you spoke? Is he still alive?" And they
said, "Your servant our father is well; he is still alive."
And they bowed down in homage. (vv. 26–28)

Joseph appears to be calm and casual as he inquires about the brothers and their father. But the moment the conversation shifts to Benjamin, he can barely contain his love and excitement.

> As he lifted his eyes and saw his brother Benjamin, his mother's son, he said, "Is this your youngest brother, of whom you spoke to me?" And he said, "May God be gracious to you, my son." (v. 29)

Without even waiting for a reply, Joseph blurts out a blessing on his younger brother. And the dam holding back Joseph's emotions cracks and quickly collapses.

Emotion

> And Joseph hurried out for he was deeply stirred over his brother, and he sought a place to weep; and he entered his chamber and wept there. (v. 30)

Later, when Joseph is finally able to control his emotions, he returns and orders the promised meal to be served (v. 31).

Fellowship

> So they served him by himself, and them by themselves, and the Egyptians, who ate with him, by themselves; because the Egyptians could not eat bread with the Hebrews, for that is loathsome to the Egyptians. Now they were seated before him, the first-born according to his birthright and the youngest according to his youth, and the men looked at one another in astonishment. (vv. 32–33)

In his commentary on Genesis, Henry Morris describes their astonishment.

> After they were assigned to seats at their table, the eleven brothers noted a remarkable thing. They had been seated in order of age, from the eldest through the youngest. If this were a mere coincidence, it was indeed marvelous. One can easily show . . . that there are no less than 39,917,000 different orders in which eleven individuals could have been seated! . . .
>
> Evidently, this man knew a great deal more about their family than they had realized; or else he had

some kind of supernatural power. They had no answer, and could only wonder about it.[4]

Then the food is served and another odd thing happens that the brothers cannot explain.

> And he took portions to them from his own table; but Benjamin's portion was five times as much as any of theirs. So they feasted and drank freely with him. (v. 34)

Everyone knew that it was taboo for an Egyptian to share a table with a Hebrew. And yet here was the prime minister of Egypt sharing the food from *his* privileged table with eleven of them. And to one, Benjamin, he bestows an even greater honor by giving him five times as much as the rest. Apparently, none of the brothers resent Joseph's attention to Benjamin, and they all relax and enjoy the meal together. One big happy family—almost.

Application and Analogy

Behind the scenes of this family reunion are two important principles that we can apply in our lives today. To help us find out what those two principles are, let's turn to Isaiah 30.

This chapter is addressed to rebellious people. In fact, they're called "rebellious children" (v. 1). God's warning to them is, "Woe to you," meaning, "as long as you're rebellious, woe to you."

When people rebel against God, many live with a sense of dread and anxiety, thinking that God is just waiting for the moment they repent so He can club them! Joseph's brothers felt and thought exactly the same things about Joseph. They returned to Egypt feeling guilty, anxious, and afraid that the moment the prime minister saw them he would imprison them or worse! But punishment is not what Joseph had planned for them, nor is it what God intends for those who return to Him.

In poetic form, verses 15–17a of Isaiah 30 describe a rebel who was running from God but has now returned, repentant. He stands naked and alone before God, like a solitary flagpole standing on a hill.[5] There he stands, with head bowed, waiting for the ax of God

---

4. Henry M. Morris, *The Genesis Record* (Grand Rapids, Mich.: Baker Book House, 1976), p. 610.

5. The Hebrew word for *flag* in Isaiah 30:17 literally means "a pole" or "a stake."

to fall on his life. Surprisingly, however, it isn't God's wrath that rains down on this person.

> Therefore the Lord longs to be gracious to you,
> And therefore He waits on high to have compassion on you.
> For the Lord is a God of justice;
> How blessed are all those who long for Him.
> (v. 18)

The Lord waits for us to quit running so He can show us His *grace*. In the same way, it wasn't Joseph's wrath that his brothers received, it was his love poured out in a gracious feast he had longed to give them.

From Isaiah's words and Joseph's example there are two things for us to remember. First, *waiting allows time for repentance.* Joseph could have revealed his identity the moment he first saw his brothers. But by waiting he has given his brothers the time they needed to have their consciences activated. Second, *waiting results in learning how to rest.* God waits for us to stop running so He can show us His grace. And we must learn that it's *only* when we stop running and wait on Him that we find rest.[6]

 Living Insights _____ STUDY ONE

Our passage today revealed deep currents of emotion running through Joseph's heart, currents that found their release only through an uncontrollable flood of tears. Look again at Genesis 43:30, reading slowly so you can capture the intensity of the scene.

> And Joseph hurried out for he was deeply stirred over his brother, and he sought a place to weep; and he entered his chamber and wept there.

Overcome with mounting emotion, Joseph, the prime minister of Egypt, all but ran from his brothers' presence as waves of sobbing came crashing through the defenses of his heart.

Passionate, unstoppable emotion isn't something you normally expect in a great leader, is it? For some reason, it's easier to dehumanize our leaders—to cast them in eight feet of cold, expressionless bronze—than to allow them the full scope of their humanness.

6. See also Isaiah 40:28–31.

- Fortunately, the Bible never denies the depth and range of the human heart. Take a moment now to examine the different emotional states of a few of God's greatest leaders.

  Moses (Num. 11:4–15) _____

  _____

  _____

  David (2 Sam. 18) _____

  _____

  _____

  Elijah (1 Kings 19:1–4) _____

  _____

  _____

  Jesus (Mark 14:32–41, Luke 22:39–46) _____

  _____

  _____

- Did the expression of these deep feelings disqualify them from leadership?

  _____

- Even if you aren't a leader, you may struggle with expressing your emotions, feeling that you are somehow not being the Christian example you should be. According to His own Word, how does God respond to our feelings?

  Psalm 34:17–18 _____

  Psalm 56:8 _____

  1 Peter 5:7 _____

  If, like Joseph, you need a place to go to pour out your heart, you *will* find a refuge in God. Won't you flee into His presence today?

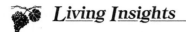 *Living Insights*

In Study One we focused on Joseph's expression of profound emotion. Next, let's take a look at the situation from his brothers' perspective.

> As [Joseph] lifted his eyes and saw his brother Benjamin, his mother's son, he said, "Is this your youngest brother, of whom you spoke to me?" And he said, "May God be gracious to you, my son." And Joseph hurried out for he was deeply stirred over his brother, and he sought a place to weep; and he entered his chamber and wept there. Then he washed his face, and came out; and he controlled himself and said, "Serve the meal." (Gen. 43:29–31)

Describe how Joseph's actions must have appeared to his brothers.

_____

_____

_____

_____

What did Joseph's brothers see concerning his emotional state?

_____

How does the brothers' perspective relate to 1 Samuel 16:7b?

_____

_____

_____

How do you think we can be more like God and look closer at a person's heart rather than the outward appearance?

_____

_____

_____

_____

Perhaps empathy is the key to unlocking another's heart. Webster defines *empathy* as "the action of understanding, being aware of, being sensitive to, and vicariously experiencing the feelings, thoughts, and experience of another of either the past or present without having the feelings, thoughts, and experience fully communicated in an objectively explicit manner."[7] How good are you at showing this tenderhearted trait to others?

_____

_____

If empathy isn't one of your strong suits, try making a monthlong commitment to studying and appropriating some of its qualities by immersing yourself in 1 Corinthians 13 and Ephesians 4:32.

7. *Webster's Ninth New Collegiate Dictionary,* see "empathy."

Chapter 9

"I AM JOSEPH!"

Genesis 44:1–45:15

No one who does a serious study of Joseph's life would deny that he was a great man. And yet he never accomplished any of the things we normally associate with biblical greatness. He never slew a giant. He never wrote a line of Scripture or made any vast prophetic predictions like Daniel. Come to think of it, Joseph never even performed a single miracle. He was just your typical boy next door, who grew up in a very troubled family.

So what made Joseph great? Why does God devote more space in Genesis to his story than to any other individual's? Because of Joseph's *attitude*, how he responded to difficult circumstances. That was the most remarkable thing about him.

American author Elbert Hubbard once wrote, "The final proof of greatness lies in being able to endure [contemptuous treatment] without resentment."[1] Joseph spent a good deal of his life enduring harsh, hateful treatment, and his attitude during those years offers indisputable proof of his greatness.

The jury is still out on his brothers, though. Thus far in the narrative, they haven't presented much evidence to prove that they share Joseph's great attitude. In Genesis 44:1–45:15, however, the brothers are about to exhibit the final proof of a great attitude— with a little help from Joseph.

The Trap: Silver in the Sack

As Joseph's feast for his brothers drew to a close (43:32–34), Joseph took his steward aside and ordered him to fill the brothers' sacks with food and put each man's money back into the mouth of his sack (44:1). But in Benjamin's sack, an additional item was stowed away: "And put my cup, the silver cup, in the mouth of the sack of the youngest" (v. 2a).

Joseph intended to use this cup as a snare, one that would bring his brothers back to him and also entrap them in an unfair situation.

---

1. Elbert Hubbard, "Get Out or Get In Line," in *Pamphlets*, Selected Writings of Elbert Hubbard, 14 vols. (New York, N.Y.: William H. Wise and Co., 1922), vol. 1, p. 58.

Why? Because he wanted to know if his brothers still saw life from a human perspective or if they had begun to develop a divine one that would enable them to see God at work even in difficult circumstances.

At dawn the next day, Joseph's brothers exchanged thanks and happily set out for home. However, just as they got outside the city, Joseph's steward overtook them and sternly accused them of stealing (vv. 3–7). The brothers were dumbfounded by the accusation and vehemently denied any wrongdoing (v. 7). In their overanxiousness to prove their innocence, though, the brothers unwittingly handed their lives over to the steward on a silver platter.

> "Behold, the money which we found in the mouth of our sacks we have brought back to you from the land of Canaan. How then could we steal silver or gold from your lord's house? With whomever of your servants it is found, let him die, and we also will be my lord's slaves." (vv. 8–9)

After adjusting the brother's promise to fit Joseph's wishes, the steward began his preplanned inspection. The cup, of course, was eventually pulled from Benjamin's sack, and the horror-stricken brothers immediately tore their clothes in an extreme gesture of grief. After reloading their grain, they sadly followed the steward back to the city (vv. 10–13).

According to the steward's bargain, however, only Benjamin had to return to Egypt. But, and note this, all the brothers returned to offer what help and defense they could. Commentator Henry Morris writes,

> This decision on their part speaks volumes about the change in character that had taken place in their lives the past twenty years, and especially in the recent period associated with the famine and their experiences in Egypt.[2]

The brothers returned to Joseph's house and immediately prostrated themselves before him (v. 14). The trap was sprung and the brothers were now caught in the jaws of an unfair circumstance.

---

2. Henry M. Morris, *The Genesis Record* (Grand Rapids, Mich.: Baker Book House, 1976), p. 615.

With a simple question, "What is this deed that you have done?" Joseph judiciously probes his brothers' attitude toward God (v. 15). Judah answered,

> "What can we say to my lord? What can we speak?
> And how can we justify ourselves? God has found
> out the iniquity of your servants." (v. 16)[3]

There it is! There's the divine perspective, the proof Joseph was looking for which would convince any jury that his brothers had become sensitive to God's hand in their daily lives.

But this was only part one of Joseph's two-part test. Now that he had tried his brothers' attitude toward God, Joseph wants to examine his brothers' care and compassion for others.

The Bargain: Brother for Brother

After demonstrating an awareness of God's hand in their lives, Judah goes on to offer all the brothers to Joseph as slaves (v. 16b). But Joseph refuses, subtly forcing his brothers to reveal their concern for others.

> But [Joseph] said, "Far be it from me to do this. The
> man in whose possession the cup has been found,
> he shall be my slave; but as for you, go up in peace
> to your father." (v. 17)

On the surface, Joseph is testing his brothers' concern and compassion for Benjamin. *"Will they dump Benjamin into my hands as callously as they dumped me into the hands of those foreign traders so many years ago?"* At the same time, he is also testing their love for Jacob. *"Are they the least bit concerned about how this will affect their father?"*

What follows in verses 18 through the end of chapter 44 is an impassioned speech that is unexcelled in all the Old Testament.

> Then Judah approached him, and said, "Oh my
> lord, may your servant please speak a word in my
> lord's ears, and do not be angry with your servant;
> for you are equal to Pharaoh. My lord asked his ser-

---

3. This is not a contrived confession about the cup. Rather, it's a genuine admission of guilt concerning what the brothers had done to Joseph years ago.

vants, saying, 'Have you a father or a brother?' And we said to my lord, 'We have an old father and a little child of his old age. Now his brother is dead, so he alone is left of his mother, and his father loves him.' Then you said to your servants, 'Bring him down to me, that I may set my eyes on him.' But we said to my lord, 'The lad cannot leave his father, for if he should leave his father, his father would die.' You said to your servants, however, 'Unless your youngest brother comes down with you, you shall not see my face again.' Thus it came about when we went up to your servant my father, we told him the words of my lord. And our father said, 'Go back, buy us a little food.' But we said, 'We cannot go down. If our youngest brother is with us, then we will go down; for we cannot see the man's face unless our youngest brother is with us.' And your servant my father said to us, 'You know that my wife bore me two sons; and the one went out from me, and I said, "Surely he is torn in pieces," and I have not seen him since. And if you take this one also from me, and harm befalls him, you will bring my gray hair down to Sheol in sorrow.'" (vv. 18–29)

Twenty years ago these same brothers had broken their father's heart with a bloodstained lie they used to cloak the truth. Now, their hearts are the ones that are breaking at the thought of causing their father any more grief. Judah continues,

"Now, therefore, when I come to your servant my father, and the lad is not with us, since his life is bound up in the lad's life, it will come about when he sees that the lad is not with us, that he will die. Thus your servants will bring the gray hair of your servant our father down to Sheol in sorrow. For your servant became surety for the lad to my father, saying, 'If I do not bring him back to you, then let me bear the blame before my father forever.' Now, therefore, please let your servant remain instead of the lad a slave to my lord, and let the lad go up with his brothers. For how shall I go up to my father if the lad is not with me, lest I see the evil that would overtake my father?" (vv. 30–34)

These are transformed men! The godly attitude of care and compassion for others is there. They have laid their hearts bare, they're deeply committed to each other, they're sorry for their previous actions, and they're passionately concerned for their father. In addition, Joseph's heart is pierced by Judah's own integrity and willingness to sacrifice his life for Benjamin's.

The Disclosure: Identity of the Governor

Joseph is overwhelmed with the proof that these are not the same brothers that sold him into bondage years ago. And now that they have passed both tests, now that their hearts are right and repentance has done its work, he can finally disclose his true identity and embrace his family.

> Then Joseph could not control himself before all those who stood by him, and he cried, "Have everyone go out from me." So there was no man with him when Joseph made himself known to his brothers. And he wept so loudly that the Egyptians heard it, and the household of Pharaoh heard of it. (45:1–2)

Imagine the confusion of the brothers. First the prime minister clears the room. They probably wondered, "What's he going to do to us?" Then he begins wailing uncontrollably right in front of them. The scene quickly deteriorates into a strange and uncomfortable one. The brothers look at each other, their questioning eyes full of fear, "Will the Egyptians think we have harmed their prime minister?" But no one dares move or say a word to this man of great power who has frightened and confused them since the day of their first visit.

Eventually, the brothers can tell that the prime minister wants to say something. But who will understand him? He doesn't speak Hebrew and none of the brothers know Egyptian. Yet, when the prime minister cries out, he speaks two words in Hebrew, *Aaa-nee Yo-saphe*, that all the brothers understand—but wished they didn't.

> Then Joseph said to his brothers, "I am Joseph!" (v. 3a)

Then Joseph immediately asks about his father, "But his brothers could not answer him, for they were dismayed at his presence" (v. 3b). Literally, it means they were terrified.

At this moment, Joseph draws his brothers near to prove his identity. "I am your brother Joseph, whom you sold into Egypt"

(v. 4). Outside of his brothers, no one but Joseph could have possibly known that terrible truth.[4]

The Response: Grace to the Guilty

Now we are going to see Joseph's own proof of greatness in his sensitive attitude toward God and his brothers.

First, Joseph shows grace and compassion to his trembling brothers. "And now do not be grieved or angry with yourselves" (v. 5a). Had we been Joseph, the first thing many of us would want to talk about is how they had wronged us and how difficult and painful our life had been as a result. But not Joseph. His first concern is to comfort his terrified and anguished brothers. Where you would expect a bitter and revengeful attitude, there is only grace and support. How was that possible? Because of Joseph's vertical perspective.

> "For God sent me before you to preserve life. For the famine has been in the land these two years, and there are still five years in which there will be neither plowing nor harvesting. And God sent me before you to preserve for you a remnant in the earth, and to keep you alive by a great deliverance." (vv. 5b–7)

In addition to showing compassion to his brothers, Joseph also generously offers to share the benefits of his being lord over Egypt.

> "Hurry and go up to my father, and say to him, 'Thus says your son Joseph, "God has made me lord of all Egypt; come down to me, do not delay. And you shall live in the land of Goshen, and you shall be near me, you and your children and your children's children and your flocks and your herds and all that you have. There I will also provide for you, for there are still five years of famine to come, lest you and your household and all that you have be impoverished."' And behold, your eyes see, and the eyes of my brother Benjamin see, that it is my mouth

4. The Hebrew term used here, na-gash, is an intimate term frequently used to indicate kissing or embracing. It's not the standard word for coming near or coming close. So why did Joseph use this term? It's possible he wanted to show his brothers that he was circumcised, which would have been irrefutable proof that he was a Jew.

which is speaking to you. Now you must tell my
father of all my splendor in Egypt, and all that you
have seen; and you must hurry and bring my father
down here." (vv. 9–13)

When there is a lack of forgiveness between two people, the
last thing either one wants is to be together, physically or emotionally. In a stirring scene of complete forgiveness, Joseph

fell on his brother Benjamin's neck and wept; and
Benjamin wept on his neck. And he kissed all his
brothers and wept on them, and afterward his brothers talked with him. (vv. 14–15)

We're not told what the brothers talked about, but there can
be little doubt that the centerpiece of attention must have been
Joseph's attitude. Throughout history many great feats have been
accomplished but none can surpass the glory and wonder of Joseph's
godly attitude at this moment.

The Truth: Lessons from the Story

This part of Joseph's story reveals at least three practical lessons
concerning our own attitude.

First, when we're able to *see* God's plan in our location—"God
sent me" (see 45:5, 7)—we are taking hold of the right attitude.
Second, when we're able to *sense* God's hand in our situation—
"God . . . made me" (45:8–9)—our attitude is moving in the right
direction. And third, when we *accept* both God's plan and God's
hand as good, even though there was evil in the process, our attitude
is just where God wants it.

Remember, true greatness is revealed, not in vast miraculous
actions, but in daily attitudes that have been shaped according to
God's perspective and compassion.

 Living Insights

Joseph's attitude in the face of contemptuous treatment was his
mark of greatness. How about your attitude? Think of one incident
of harsh treatment you have had to endure, and write down how
you responded to it.

Incident: _____

_____

Response: _____

_____

What did your response reveal about your attitude?

_____

_____

Of the three areas of attitude we concluded our lesson with, which is the weakest in your life?

☐ Seeing God's plan

☐ Sensing God's hand

☐ Accepting both as good, even though evil may be involved in the process

Take time now to brainstorm ways to strengthen that area. Also be thinking of how you can apply one of these ideas this week.

_____

_____

_____

 Living Insights   STUDY TWO

When you enter the green tranquility of a quiet park, or still your soul by the shore of a serene mountain lake, do you ever notice the reflected loveliness of the trees in the calm water? The leaves shimmer and float, and the tips of the trees lap the water's edge, almost lulling you into believing that this watery world is the best of all worlds.

Almost . . . until the surface is disturbed, and the reflected image ripples away and disappears in fluid fragments. Only then do you look up and see the splendid reality that was only dimly water-colored on the canvas of the lake.

Like the lake's surface, Joseph is merely the lovely reflection of a more splendid reality, Jesus Christ. Let's use our time today to see how Joseph's life reflected that of our Lord Jesus. Look up the following passages and write down the similarities you find between the two men as well as any insights you discover along the way.

Genesis 37:3 _____

Matthew 3:17 _____

Insight _____

Genesis 39:7–12 _____

Luke 4:1–13, Hebrews 4:15 _____

Insight _____

Genesis 39:20, 41:39–43 _____

Philippians 2:5–11 _____

Insight _____

Genesis 45:5, 7 _____

John 3:16, 11:49–52 _____

Insight _____

Genesis 50:15–21 _____

Ephesians 1:7, John 3:17, 1 John 1:9 _____

Insight _____

Genesis 45:9–11, 47:27 _____

John 14:2–3, Revelation 21 _____

Insight _____

Chapter 10

THE ULTIMATE FAMILY REUNION

Genesis 45:16–46:7, 28–30

*F*amily *reunion.* That's still a potent phrase that evokes many wonderful images in people's minds. Images of bulging pies and pudgy uncles or of chunky potato salads and chubby babies.

But not all reunions are well-orchestrated family conventions everyone knows about a year in advance. Sometimes they occur, well . . . totally unplanned, unannounced, and unanticipated. Just ask Robert Shafran. He simply enrolled as a freshman at Sullivan County Community College in upstate New York, and suddenly,

> "Guys were slapping me on the back, and girls were hugging and kissing me," he recalls. It was very nice, but they kept calling him Eddy. A sophomore at Sullivan, Michael Domnitz, whose best friend, Eddy Galland, had just transferred to Nassau Community College on Long Island, cleared up the mystery. After learning that Shafran was born the same day as Galland—July 12, 1961—and that he, like Eddy, was adopted, Domnitz got the two young men together for a meeting. They found they laughed alike and talked alike. Their birthmarks and their IQs (148) were identical. . . . Hospital records confirmed what the boys already knew, and the New York press trumpeted the story of reunited twins.
>
> Then the unbelievable happened. David Kellman, a freshman at New York's Queens College who had seen their picture in the paper, called the Galland household. "You're not going to believe this," he began—and, indeed, only documents at Manhattan's Louise Wise adoption agency made it credible. Robert, David and Eddy are triplets, born in that order, within 27 minutes of each other.[1]

---

1. Judy Gould, "What Happens When Three Young Men Find Out They're Triplets? It's Not as Simple as 1-2-3," *People,* October 13, 1980, p. 86.

In our last lesson we saw Joseph's brothers experience an unplanned, unannounced, and unexpected reunion of their own.
Today, these same brothers are going to travel back to their father
in Canaan with news of this incredible event and with Joseph's
offer to host a permanent family reunion in Egypt (Gen. 45:9–13).
"Dad, you're not going to believe this," you can almost hear them
say—and, indeed, only the evidence of the goods Joseph sends with
his brothers will make their story credible.

Plans for the Reunion

When we left Joseph and his brothers in Genesis 45:15, they
were weeping and talking together as a family. And while they
talked, tongues wagged along the royal Egyptian grapevine about
an unplanned, unannounced, and unexpected family reunion over
in the prime minister's house.

Pharaoh's Acceptance

> Now when the news was heard in Pharaoh's house
> that Joseph's brothers had come, it pleased Pharaoh
> and his servants. Then Pharaoh said to Joseph, "Say
> to your brothers, 'Do this: load your beasts and go
> to the land of Canaan, and take your father and
> your households and come to me, and I will give
> you the best of the land of Egypt and you shall eat
> the fat of the land.' Now you are ordered, 'Do this:
> take wagons from the land of Egypt for your little
> ones and for your wives, and bring your father and
> come. And do not concern yourselves with your
> goods, for the best of all the land of Egypt is yours.' "
> (vv. 16–20)

By divine providence, Pharaoh not only endorses Joseph's plan
to bring his family to Egypt, but he also graciously supplies the
wagons that will speed the return of Joseph's aging father.

Joseph's Provisions

The wagons are quickly rounded up, and Joseph begins outfitting
his brothers with provisions and presents.

> To each of them he gave changes of garments, but
> to Benjamin he gave three hundred pieces of silver
> and five changes of garments. And to his father he

sent as follows: ten donkeys loaded with the best things of Egypt, and ten female donkeys loaded with grain and bread and sustenance for his father on the journey. So he sent his brothers away, and as they departed, he said to them, "Do not quarrel on the journey." (vv. 22–24)

"Do not quarrel." The Hebrew term Joseph uses is *ragaz*, meaning "to be agitated or perturbed," and it is often the last step before a fight breaks out. Joseph knows his brothers. Even though they have just repented and feel close to one another, he also knows that sudden wealth can do terrible things to a family. And he also knows the awful power of jealousy firsthand.

Jacob's Response

Fortunately, the brothers' trip to Canaan isn't marred by any squabbles over possessions. Their minds are probably too frenzied trying to figure out how they will explain Joseph to their father. "Dad, you're not going to believe this," they plan to say—and poor old Jacob doesn't.

Then they went up from Egypt, and came to the land of Canaan to their father Jacob. And they told him, saying, "Joseph is still alive, and indeed he is ruler over all the land of Egypt." But he was stunned, for he did not believe them. (vv. 25–26)

The Hebrew literally says, "his heart grew numb." His sons want him to exhume a hope he had buried in his mind years ago. "Joseph, alive?" Jacob remembers the bloody coat and feels the weight of all the years of missing and mourning his precious son. "Joseph, alive? No, it's impossible!"

Jacob's sons sense their mistake. They have given their father too much information too fast. So they back up and begin again, this time carefully bringing forth every proof they can think of to support their fantastic claims.

When they told him all the words of Joseph that he had spoken to them, and when he saw the wagons that Joseph had sent to carry him, the spirit of their father Jacob revived. (v. 27)

With the hope he had buried long ago now resurrected, Jacob catches his breath and tells his anxious sons,

"It is enough; my son Joseph is still alive. I will go and see him before I die." (v. 28)

Journey from Canaan to Egypt

Looking at Jacob's situation, you almost feel like you're watching the pilot program to the old TV series "The Beverly Hillbillies." The show's song describes Jed's good fortune, but in the Genesis version, it also describes Jacob's. "Well, the first thing you know, ol' Jacob's a millionaire. Kinfolk said, 'Jacob move away from there.' Said, 'Land of Egypt is the place you oughta be,' so he loaded up his carts, and moved to . . ." well, a Beverly Hills of his own in Egypt.

But it's more than just Jacob and his immediate family who are pulling up their tent pegs and moving. The whole nation of Israel is packing to follow Jacob. To signify this, Jacob is referred to in Genesis 46:1 by his national title, Israel, instead of his personal name.

That Jacob was about to see his long-lost son doesn't change the fact that moves are tough. They're physically demanding and fraught with uncertainties and feelings of insecurity. No doubt Jacob feels a heavy responsibility about transplanting his family from their comfortable roots in Canaan to the foreign soil of Egypt. His little nation is about to cross over into a fast-paced, polytheistic society that could swallow them whole.

It's not surprising to read, then, that just before Jacob leaves the borders of his own land, he stops to seek God's assurance on whether to proceed or not.

> So Israel set out with all that he had, and came to Beersheba, and offered sacrifices to the God of his father Isaac. And God spoke to Israel in visions of the night and said, "Jacob, Jacob." And he said, "Here I am." And He said, "I am God, the God of your father; do not be afraid to go down to Egypt, for I will make you a great nation there. I will go down with you to Egypt, and I will also surely bring you up again; and Joseph will close your eyes." (46:1–4)

The one thing Jacob needed to hear, God says, and more— much more.[2] Israel went to sleep afraid and unsure, but when he

---

2. First the Lord revealed Himself to Jacob, "I am God" (v. 3a). Next, He relieved Jacob's fears, "Do not be afraid to go" (v. 3b). Then He promised to make Jacob into a great nation and assured him that He would go with them (v. 3c–4a). And, finally, God promised to bring Jacob's ancestors out of Egypt (v. 4b)—a direct prophecy concerning the exodus Moses would lead four hundred years later.

awakens the next morning, he is confident and eager to get underway. "God is with us; He's going to make us into a great nation; I'm going to see Joseph!"

Reunion with Joseph

Israel was only seventy-strong when they came plodding into Egypt (v. 27b). Just a pebble of a nation that would one day bruise Pharaoh's heel enough times to be returned to Canaan about two million strong. But for now they're just a backwoods clan plodding past the stares of snooty Egyptians. They aren't even sure where they're supposed to go. So Jacob sends Judah ahead to ask Joseph for directions, and they eventually arrive at their new home in Goshen (v. 28). And it isn't long before Jacob feels the embrace of his favorite son.

> And Joseph prepared his chariot and went up to Goshen to meet his father Israel; as soon as he appeared before him, he fell on his neck and wept on his neck a long time. Then Israel said to Joseph, "Now let me die, since I have seen your face, that you are still alive." (vv. 29–30)

In those tears, this aged father and favored son wrung out buckets of emotion that had been bottled up in their hearts for the past twenty years.

 Living Insights

The reunion of Jacob and Joseph is only one of several great reunions mentioned in Scripture, each of which foreshadows the greatest of all: when believers will be gathered to Jesus to spend eternity with Him. Let's look at a few of these reunions, noting the specifics—whether they're spiritual, emotional, relational, or anything else—that might give us a glimpse of our ultimate reunion in heaven.

- The reunion of the exiles in Jerusalem (Nehemiah 8):

  _____

  _____

  _____

- The reunion of the prodigal son and his father (Luke 15:11–24):

  _____

  _____

  _____

- Paul's brief reunion with the Ephesian elders (Acts 20:17–38):

  _____

  _____

  _____

Now step out of the shadows and peer into the heavenlies through the windows of 1 Thessalonians 4:13–18 and Revelation 21. Isn't it nice to know that this reunion will never end but last throughout all eternity?

Living Insights   STUDY TWO

Let's reread God's words of comfort to Jacob as this well-traveled patriarch faced the last move of his life.

> And God spoke to Israel in visions of the night and said, "Jacob, Jacob." And he said, "Here I am." And He said, "I am God, the God of your father; do not be afraid to go down to Egypt, for I will make you a great nation there. I will go down with you to Egypt, and I will also surely bring you up again; and Joseph will close your eyes." (Gen. 46:2–4)

What do the Lord's words reveal about His character?

_____

_____

_____

_____

_____

How does God respond to Jacob's fear?

_____

_____

_____

_____

How are we to respond to God when we are afraid (see Ps. 46)?

_____

_____

_____

_____

Look up Genesis 46:5–7. What do Jacob's actions here teach you about how to respond to God's voice?

_____

_____

_____

_____

If you're feeling afraid and uncertain, won't you follow Jacob's example by seeking the Lord and taking Him at His word (see Luke 11:9–13, Deut. 31:6, Ps. 119:105, Phil. 4:6–7)?

Chapter 11

EFFICIENCY IN BUSINESS THEN AND NOW
Genesis 46:31–47:26

D o you remember Robert Louis Stevenson's fascinating novel about human nature titled *Dr. Jekyll and Mr. Hyde?* The story revolves around the strange case of a kindly scientist, Dr. Jekyll, who by night transformed himself into the wholly evil Mr. Hyde.

It's a great piece of science fiction. Or is it so fictional? Haven't you known some religious Jekylls, who faithfully attend church, serve on boards, and teach Sunday School. But come Monday morning it's not Dr. Jekyll who shows up for work—it's Mr. Hyde.

In Stevenson's book, the villainous Hyde stalked the dark labyrinths of London's lamplit streets. Today's Mr. Hydes, however, are much different. As C. S. Lewis wrote,

> I live in the Managerial Age, in a world of "Admin."
> The greatest evil is not now done in those sordid
> "dens of crime" that Dickens loved to paint. It is not
> done in concentration camps and labour camps. In
> those we see its final result. But it is conceived and
> ordered (moved, seconded, carried and minuted) in
> clean, carpeted, warmed and well-lighted offices, by
> quiet men with white collars and cut fingernails and
> smooth-shaven cheeks who do not need to raise their
> voice.[1]

Christianity gets trampled underfoot more often by the Jekyll-and-Hyde types than by practically anyone else. Yet very little is said from the pulpit about the Christian's Monday-through-Friday occupational life, even though it is there that the world receives its greatest exposure to the Christian faith.

Some General Observations about Business

To begin our study, let's focus on three very important observations concerning work and how it affects our Christian witness.

1. C. S. Lewis, *The Screwtape Letters* (New York, N.Y.: Macmillan Publishing Co., 1961), p. 10.

First: *The way we do our work is a revealing display of character.* It's not what we wear or how we act on Sundays that demonstrates to the world our credibility as Christians; it's the way we behave on the job. If you were to ask others who work with you to critique your character, they aren't going to talk about the Sunday you; they're going to evaluate the nine-to-five you.

What kind of character traits do you display at work? Are you diligent or lazy? Truthful or dishonest? Do you gossip and sow discord or are you loyal and enthusiastic? Would your coworkers say you're patient and cooperative or impatient and cantankerous?

Second: *Work is a demanding arena of pressure.* Every job has its own unique set of pressures. In some jobs it's a demanding boss or a relentless deadline. In others it's the pressures of cutthroat inter-office jealousies, competition, or too much work and not enough people. In these pressure-cooker situations our true character, not just what we say we believe, is paraded in front of everyone. When the heat in the kitchen gets unbearable, do you let off steam like everyone else around you, or do you let in a breeze of fresh air?

Third: *Work is an exacting test of our efficiency.* It helps us see how organized and decisive we are, how thorough we are when it comes to the tasks before us, how willing we are to be accountable, how perceptive we are in spotting and correcting potential problems, and how resourceful we are in correcting them. How would you rate *your* efficiency at work? How organized are you? How decisive? How thorough?

For the past several lessons we have focused on Joseph's relationship with his family. We have seen his divine perspective and many godly qualities. But what about the nine-to-five Joseph? What kind of character traits does this top executive reflect Monday through Friday? Does Joseph use the pressures of Egypt's food crisis as an excuse for becoming an occupational Mr. Hyde?

A Specific Example

Let's observe Joseph's example as he handles Egypt's famine and Israel's resettlement.

> And Joseph said to his brothers and to his father's household, "I will go up and tell Pharaoh, and will say to him, 'My brothers and my father's household, who were in the land of Canaan, have come to me; and the men are shepherds, for they have been keep-

ers of livestock; and they have brought their flocks and their herds and all that they have.' And it shall come about when Pharaoh calls you and says, 'What is your occupation?' that you shall say, 'Your servants have been keepers of livestock from our youth even until now, both we and our fathers,' that you may live in the land of Goshen; for every shepherd is loathsome to the Egyptians." (vv. 31–34)

It would be easy for Joseph to assume that Pharaoh will give his family whichever tract of land he requests. "After all," Joseph could think, "Pharaoh owes me. I'm the one who saved Egypt from withering away in this famine." But Joseph doesn't attempt to secure a place for his family by presuming upon his relationship with Pharaoh or his position as prime minister. Instead, he employs the first of several efficient business principles.

He Planned Ahead with Wise Objectivity

As a slave, a prisoner, and prime minister, Joseph has studied the Egyptian mind. He has learned how to live and work in a culture different from his own. And when it comes to integrating his family into this society, Joseph uses this understanding to implement some wise and objective plans. He discusses with his family his plan to report to Pharaoh (v. 31). He thinks objectively about how Jewish shepherds will be viewed by Egyptians (v. 34b). He even has his family rehearse what they will say when questioned (v. 34).

In his book *Excellence in Leadership,* Frank Goble notes,

> Excellent leaders have the ability to see things realistically. They are not easily deceived by others, nor do they practice self-deception.[2]

Joseph saw things realistically. He didn't indulge in any deceptions about the differences between his father's culture and Pharaoh's. On the contrary, his objective appraisal enabled him to safely navigate his family's passage into the peaceful harbor of Goshen.

Before the family finally meets Pharaoh, however, Joseph demonstrates a second desirable trait of an efficient prime minister.

---

2. Frank Goble, *Excellence in Leadership* (Thornwood, N.Y.: Caroline House Publishers, 1972), p. 131.

He Submitted to Authority with Loyal Accountability

According to Genesis 47:1–2, Joseph updates Pharaoh on his family's arrival and introduces five of his brothers. Pharaoh discusses the brothers' future and concludes their interview by saying, "The land of Egypt is at your disposal" (v. 6). Joseph then sets up another appointment in which his father meets and blesses Pharaoh (v. 7). The outcome couldn't have been more favorable.

> Joseph settled his father and his brothers, and gave them a possession in the land of Egypt, in the best of the land, in the land of Rameses. (v. 11)

Through all of this, Joseph reflects a beautiful blend of humility and integrity. He is a competent and disciplined leader who works cooperatively with his boss. Nowhere does Joseph give the slightest hint that he resists being accountable to Pharaoh. In fact, Joseph *wants* Pharaoh to know what is going on. Everything is done completely aboveboard so there will be no surprises, no after-the-fact revelations, that will cause Pharaoh to doubt Joseph's loyalty.

In verse 13, the focus shifts from his family to the famine.

> Now there was no food in all the land, because the famine was very severe, so that the land of Egypt and the land of Canaan languished because of the famine. And Joseph gathered all the money that was found in the land of Egypt and in the land of Canaan for the grain which they bought, and Joseph brought the money into Pharaoh's house. And when the money was all spent in the land of Egypt and in the land of Canaan, all the Egyptians came to Joseph and said, "Give us food, for why should we die in your presence? For our money is gone." (vv. 13–15)

The people are caught in a vise-like grip of starvation and desperation. Joseph has the power to tighten that grip or loosen it since he carries the key to the granaries. It would be so easy for him to take advantage of the people. Yet he chooses to demonstrate a third characteristic of an efficient businessman.

He Arranged for Survival with Personal Integrity

Joseph brings *all* the money into Pharaoh's house (v. 14). He doesn't pilfer, falsify any records, or extort a little extra on the side for himself. He turns it all in. That's integrity.

> Year after year businessmen study college records,
> screen applicants, and offer special inducement to
> proven people. What are they after, really? Brains?
> Energy? Know-how? These things are desirable, sure.
> But they will carry a man so far. If he is to move to
> the top and be entrusted with command decisions,
> there must be a plus factor, something that takes
> mere ability and doubles or trebles its effectiveness.
> To describe this magic characteristic there is only
> one word: *integrity.*[3]

Undergirding Joseph's integrity are the same two qualities he
had once advised Pharaoh that a man in his position should possess
(see Gen. 41:33–35). Joseph is *discerning,* perceptive of what is
going to happen before the fact; and he is *wise,* a builder who uses
his knowledge for constructive purposes. Because of this, the people
are not hesitant to come to him for food when they exhaust all
their money.

> Then Joseph said, "Give up your livestock, and I will
> give you food for your livestock, since your money
> is gone." So they brought their livestock to Joseph,
> and Joseph . . . fed them with food in exchange for
> all their livestock that year. And when that year was
> ended, they came to him the next year and said to
> him, "We will not hide from my lord that our money
> is all spent, and the cattle are my lord's. There is
> nothing left for my lord except our bodies and our
> lands. Why should we die before your eyes, both we
> and our land? Buy us and our land for food, and we
> and our land will be slaves to Pharaoh. So give us
> seed, that we may live and not die, and that the
> land may not be desolate." (47:16–19)

Joseph does everything he can to uphold the people's dignity.
When their monetary system collapses, he opens the door for them
to trade their livestock for food. Even so, it isn't long before this
means of payment becomes exhausted and Joseph's character is
tested again. But just when many might have thought about aban-
doning ship, Joseph sets his mind to reconstructing a better boat.

---

3. Arthur Gordon, quoted by Goble in *Excellence in Leadership,* p. 129.

He Accepted the Challenge with Innovative Creativity

> So Joseph bought all the land of Egypt for
> Pharaoh, for every Egyptian sold his field, because
> the famine was severe upon them. Thus the land
> became Pharaoh's. And as for the people, he re-
> moved them to the cities from one end of Egypt's
> border to the other. Only the land of the priests he
> did not buy, for the priests had an allotment from
> Pharaoh, and they lived off the allotment which
> Pharaoh gave them. Therefore, they did not sell
> their land. Then Joseph said to the people, "Behold,
> I have today bought you and your land for Pharaoh;
> now, here is seed for you, and you may sow the
> land." (vv. 20–23)

Every challenge in leadership is a call to arms of innovative
thinking. In Joseph's case, he paid the people for their lands, strategically moved them to cities for their survival, and gave them
seed to sow. Again the people were allowed to work, thus preserving
their personal integrity and national unity. Next, Joseph devises a
one-fifth levy for Pharaoh and allows the people to keep the rest for
their survival (v. 24). The people's response gushes with gratitude.

> "You have saved our lives! Let us find favor in the
> sight of my lord, and we will be Pharaoh's slaves."
> (v. 25)

What started out as simply a creative idea became a successful
statute that safely navigated the Egyptian empire through the turbulence of famine (v. 26).[4]

Some Helpful Suggestions

If you were to place the private Joseph beside the prime minister
Joseph, their portraits would look exactly the same. Joseph is not

---

4. Joseph is a great model of efficiency, but there is one even greater. All four principles
from Joseph's life can be found at the Cross. First, God the Father planned ahead with wise
objectivity. He saw us as we were—lost, sinful, and undone. Next, Jesus Christ submitted
to the Father's authority with loyal accountability and took on human flesh to bring us the
good news of salvation. Throughout the years that Jesus lived and arranged for our survival,
He was the paragon of personal integrity. And lastly, God met the challenge of saving
mankind with the creative and innovative plan of a virgin birth, a sinless life, a sinless
sacrifice, an unexpected resurrection, and the promise of a joyous second coming.

your religious Dr. Jekyll who takes on a Mr. Hyde personality when he dons official robes. If we're to avoid the Jekyll-and-Hyde syndrome and live more like Joseph, we must cling to character even in the most famishing of circumstances.

Of utmost importance to every believer must be a commitment to Christian principles. Compromising over matters of basic strategy may be wise. But compromising over biblical principles is not. It can lead only to a bankrupt life.

Another priority for the Christian is the careful investment of time. Peter Drucker writes,

> Nothing else perhaps distinguishes effective executives as much as their tender loving care of time. . . . [Without this] no amount of ability, skill, experience, or knowledge will make an executive effective.[5]

Lastly, we must seek to maintain the purest motives behind our dealings with people. A constant vigil must be kept over our hearts by asking ourselves, "Why am I saying or doing this?

In Stevenson's science fiction story, a potion changed Dr. Jekyll into the hideous Mr. Hyde. In reality, all it takes is a mixture of impure motives and improper priorities.

 Living Insights   STUDY ONE

Our lesson today shows that our behavior at work puts not only our character on display but also Christianity itself. How are you doing in this important realm of your life? Take some time now to give yourself a checkup by answering the following questions.

What are some of the pressures and demands you face at work?

_____

_____

_____

_____

_____

5. Quoted by Goble in *Excellence in Leadership*, p. 140.

What kind of character traits do you display in dealing with these pressures?

_____

_____

_____

For just a moment, step out of your shoes and into your coworkers'. How do you think they would describe what it's like to work with you?

_____

_____

_____

_____

_____

Do you see any places that need improvement—perhaps an area involving efficiency, planning, accountability, integrity, or creativity? Write down what that area is on a three-by-five card, keeping it where you can see it at work, and commit yourself to praying about it this week.

 Living Insights

In his book _Decision Making and the Will of God,_ Garry Friesen devotes an entire section to giving scriptural explanation for God's will and the Christian's work. Here are some of his conclusions.

Our work should be marked by: sincerity of heart (Eph. 6:5), enthusiasm and diligence (Eph. 6:6), reverence and devotion to Christ (Col. 3:22–23), good will (Eph. 6:7), discipline (2 Thess. 3:11), quietness (2 Thess. 3:12), cooperation (Titus 2:9), honesty (Titus 2:10), integrity (Eph. 6:6), efficiency (Eph. 5:16), gratitude (Col. 3:17), and generosity (Eph. 4:28).

Our goal should be: to earn our own food (2 Thess. 3:10), to provide adequately for our own family (1 Tim. 5:8), to behave properly toward outsiders (1 Thess. 4:11–12), to avoid being a burden to others (2 Thess. 3:8), to earn enough to meet our needs and to contribute toward others' needs (Eph. 4:28), to set a good example for others (2 Thess. 3:9), to preserve God's reputation (1 Tim. 6:1), and to adorn the doctrine of God so that there is no discrepancy between profession and practice (Titus 2:10).

In relationship to our employer, we should: be submissive and obedient, as unto the Lord (Eph. 6:5, Col. 3:22); be diligent in our work, with the idea that our ultimate superior is the Lord (Eph. 6:6–8); work as hard when no one is watching as we do under direct supervision (Eph. 6:6); regard our employer as worthy of all honor (1 Tim. 6:1); show respect even to those supervisors who are unreasonable (1 Pet. 2:18); and not take advantage of a Christian employer, but serve all the more out of love (1 Tim. 6:2).

In relation to our employees, we should: not abuse our workers (Eph. 6:9); treat our employees with justice and fairness (Col. 4:1); apply the golden rule, treating our workers as we would wish to be treated (Eph. 6:9); be fair and prompt in the payment of wages (James 5:4); and remember that we are accountable to God, the Master of all, for the treatment of our workers (Col. 4:1).[6]

What is your work marked by?

_____

_____

_____

Which of the qualities under the first category of Friesen's list are most absent from your work?

_____

_____

_____

What are your goals at work? (List in real, not theoretical order of importance.)

1. _____

2. _____

3. _____

6. Garry Friesen, *Decision Making and the Will of God* (Portland, Oreg.: Multnomah Press, 1980), pp. 337–38.

How pure are your motives and how right are your means for achieving those goals?

Motives: _____

Means: _____

On a one-to-ten scale, ten being best, how would you evaluate your relationship with your employer? _____

Using Friesen's list as a reference, what could you do to move that up a notch higher?

_____

_____

_____

How would you evaluate your relationships with those who work under you? _____

From Friesen's list, what could you do to improve those relationships?

_____

_____

_____

_____

Chapter 12

HIGHLIGHTS OF TWILIGHT AND MIDNIGHT

Genesis 47:29–31; 50:15–21

From the pit of despair in Canaan to the pinnacle of success in Egypt, our sojourn in Joseph's life has been nothing short of incredible—and exhausting.

We boarded Joseph's biography when he was a teenager and have been on a nonstop roller-coaster ride ever since. It began with a smooth journey into Dothan where we suddenly plunged into a pit and shot back out again into a wrenching ninety-degree turn toward Egypt. There God's blessings quickly took hold and we began a steady, clickity-clack ascent following Joseph, Potiphar's personal steward. At the top, we met a real screamer—Mrs. Potiphar! She spun us around and hurled us headlong into a dark Egyptian dungeon. Inside we bottomed out, started to climb, interpreted a dream, and then nose-dived into forgetfulness.

By Pharaoh's order and God's grace, we then blasted off into an ear-popping ascent from prisoner to prime minister. Cresting this position we plowed into ten brothers, heard a jolting accusation, then shot out in a loop to Canaan for Benjamin and back again to Egypt. From there we careened through a few unexpected twists and turns as Joseph put his brothers to the test. After that, we rounded another curve with incredible g-force.

It began with Joseph revealing his identity, and his brothers feeling pinned to the floor by the crushing guilt-force of their own consciences. Joseph's grace and forgiveness eased us out of that curve straight into a second loop, this time to pick up Joseph's father and the Israelite nation. Swinging down from Canaan, we met Joseph for a heart-stopping reunion with his aged father. Finally, the brakes began to take hold and we slowed as Joseph helped his family glide safely past Pharaoh into Goshen where they survived the famine crisis.

Kind of makes you tired, doesn't it? And it's not over yet! As we visit Joseph and his family for the last time, seventeen years have passed since Jacob and Joseph were reunited. Jacob is now 147 years old and he's tired. It's a good tired, though. He's back with

Joseph where God wants him to be, and his tiny nation is having a baby boom (Gen. 47:27–28).

Jacob: Sickness, Blessing, and Death

Beginning in Genesis 47:29, our narrative slows again with an intimate scene of Jacob preparing for his reunion with his forefathers.

> When the time for Israel to die drew near, he called his son Joseph and said to him, "Please, if I have found favor in your sight, place now your hand under my thigh and deal with me in kindness and faithfulness. Please do not bury me in Egypt, but when I lie down with my fathers, you shall carry me out of Egypt and bury me in their burial place." And he said, "I will do as you have said." And he said, "Swear to me." So he swore to him. Then Israel bowed in worship at the head of the bed. (vv. 29–31)

In a touching exchange, Joseph gives his word to his father, and Jacob gives his son the lasting memory of a father who worshiped.

Jacob with Joseph's Sons

As we move on, the brakes are quickly applied again, and we come upon Jacob's blessing of Joseph's sons, Manasseh and Ephraim. First, the ailing patriarch reminisces (48:1–5, 7); then he calls his grandsons, now in their twenties, to his side to bless them (vv. 8–20).

As Gary Smalley and John Trent point out in *The Blessing*, there is something more being passed on here than just a theological promise to the nation of Israel.

> In addition to the unique spiritual meanings attached to the family blessing, the blessing always has had an intensely personal side to it as well. . . .
>
> The personal, or relational, side of using the blessing to communicate parental love and acceptance is what orthodox Jewish homes have continued to practice in blessing children. While they recognize the unique spiritual and prophetic aspects of the blessing the patriarchs gave their children, they adopted the basic relationship elements of the blessing laid down in the Scriptures to encourage

their children. These tools communicate acceptance and affirmation and still apply to men and women today.[1]

While the theological aspects of patriarchal blessing are not being passed on anymore, the need to pass on unconditional acceptance and approval is just as important a blessing today as it was then.

Jacob with His Sons

Crossing over into Genesis 49, we see the dying patriarch gathering his sons to make specific predictions concerning each one (vv. 1–27). In conclusion, Jacob charges them with his funeral arrangements (vv. 29–32), then breathes his last (v. 33).

Jacob's Death and Joseph's Mourning

Jacob was with Joseph the first seventeen years of his son's life. And by God's grace, Joseph was able to be with his father for the last seventeen years of his. Now, however, for the second time in his life, Joseph experiences the wrenching pain of separation and loss.

> Then Joseph fell on his father's face, and wept over him and kissed him. And Joseph commanded his servants the physicians to embalm his father. So the physicians embalmed Israel. Now forty days were required for it, for such is the period required for embalming. And the Egyptians wept for him seventy days.[2] (50:1–3)

Joseph: Grief, Grace, Glory

Joseph's narrative has slowed to the mournful cadence of a funeral procession. But a surprising turn of grace still lies ahead.

Burial of His Father

With Pharaoh's permission, Joseph goes up with a great company of chariots and horsemen to the cave of Machpelah in Canaan and buries his father (vv. 4–14). Joyce Baldwin explains why Joseph didn't settle for Forest Lawn on the Nile.

1. Gary Smalley and John Trent, *The Blessing* (Nashville, Tenn.: Thomas Nelson Publishers, 1986), pp. 22–23.

2. In her commentary *The Message of Genesis 12–50,* Joyce Baldwin explains that "public mourning for a Pharaoh did not last longer than seventy-two days, so Jacob/Israel was greatly honoured." (Downers Grove, Ill.: InterVarsity Press, 1986), p. 215.

Despite the prominence of Joseph in the government of Egypt, the family would never consider its inheritance to be in Egypt. The legitimacy of their claim to Canaan lay with the divine gift of the land to Abraham, the first forefather of Israel. . . . The return of the funeral cortège from Egypt for Jacob's burial there renewed the family's claim to the cave, and also to the land. It was a pledge that they would one day return to occupy what had in fact been bestowed on Abraham and Sarah, Isaac and Rebekah. Leah too was buried there (but not Rachel), and Jacob would take his place in the family mausoleum, as one of the three great names for ever associated with God's promise of the land: Abraham, Isaac and Jacob.[3]

Forgiveness of His Brothers

In the wake of Jacob's death, Joseph's brothers feel something more than loss, they begin to feel the prickling stings of fear.

When Joseph's brothers saw that their father was dead, they said, "What if Joseph should bear a grudge against us and pay us back in full for all the wrong which we did to him!" So they sent a message to Joseph, saying, "Your father charged before he died, saying, 'Thus you shall say to Joseph, "Please forgive, I beg you, the transgression of your brothers and their sin, for they did you wrong."' And now, please forgive the transgression of the servants of the God of your father." (vv. 15–17a)

The brothers fear Joseph's wrath. According to verse 18, they even go so far as to throw themselves at Joseph's feet, promising to be his servants in order to win his mercy. But the brothers' groveling doesn't appeal to Joseph; it just makes him weep (v. 17b).

At this moment, the brothers aren't sure whether or not their lives are about to take a dive into a dungeon. But Joseph quickly assuages their fears with these words of forgiveness and grace.

But Joseph said to them, "Do not be afraid, for am I in God's place? And as for you, you meant evil

---

3. Baldwin, *The Message of Genesis 12–50*, p. 214.

against me, but God meant it for good in order to bring about this present result, to preserve many people alive. So therefore, do not be afraid; I will provide for you and your little ones." So he comforted them and spoke kindly to them. (vv. 19–21)

Completion of His Life

How Joseph's family and friends must have enjoyed the pleasure of his company! Instead of nursing old, bitter wounds, Joseph freely extended grace from an open hand. He led . . . remembered . . . spoke . . . and forgave by grace. Grace enabled Joseph to enjoy his twilight years as a granddad and a great granddad (vv. 22–23). And Joseph's last recorded words imparted grace and encouragement to his brothers, reminding them of God's tender faithfulness.

And Joseph said to his brothers, "I am about to die, but God will surely take care of you, and bring you up from this land to the land which He promised on oath to Abraham, to Isaac and to Jacob. Then Joseph made the sons of Israel swear, saying, "God will surely take care of you, and you shall carry my bones up from here." So Joseph died at the age of one hundred and ten years; and he was embalmed and placed in a coffin in Egypt. (vv. 24–26).

Today: Our Final Years

Though we've come to the end of Joseph's story, the legacy of his life lingers on. Here are just two important lessons for us to remember. First, *to grow old free of bitterness is one of the finest gifts we can leave humanity.* What memory will your children have of you? Will it be of someone who constantly complained and picked at the scabs of the past? Or will it be of someone with joy in their heart like Joseph, whose whole life was seasoned with God's grace?

Second, *to face death, right with God and man, is the finest way we can enter eternity.* The grace and forgiveness that permeated Joseph's life weren't manufactured by simply looking inward, to himself. They resulted from looking outward, to God.

Have you been looking in all the wrong places to find a right relationship with God? If so, take a moment to allow Him to redirect your search (read Rom. 3:23; 6:23; 5:8, and 5:1–2). How about your relationships with others? Do they need redirecting also?

Chances are, if your relationship with God is out of kilter, so are your relationships with others (read 1 John 2:9–11, 4:20).

 Living Insights

Joseph left his loved ones the fragrant legacy of a life lived in grace. Have you thought about the legacy you will leave behind? Quiet your heart now, and ponder the words of one author who has considered what a precious gift remembrances can be.

> What pictures will *my* son . . . my daughters
> remember? . . .
>
> I've resolved to give fewer lectures,
>> to send fewer platitudes rolling their way,
>> to give less criticism,
>> to offer fewer opinions. . . .
>
> From now on, I'll give them pictures they can
>> live by,
>> pictures that can comfort them,
>> encourage them,
>> and keep them warm
>> in my absence.
>
> Because when I'm gone, there will only be
>> silence.
>> And memories. . . .
>
> Of all
>> I could give
>> to make their lives a little fuller,
>> a little richer,
>> a little more prepared
>> for the journey ahead of them,
>> nothing compares to the gift of
>>> remembrance—
>> pictures that show they are special
>> and that they are loved.
>
> Pictures that will be there
>> when I am not.

Pictures that have within them
a redemption all their own.[4]

Describe a few pictures your children will have of you in their mental scrapbooks after you are gone.

1. _____

_____

2. _____

_____

3. _____

_____

Living Insights

Joseph's legacy went far beyond those whose lives he touched during his lifetime. His legacy has touched us as well. Take time now to write down from each chapter some of the truths and insights you have gleaned about this man of grace and truth.

Joseph: From Pit to Pinnacle

1. Favored Son, Hated Brother _____

_____

2. Resisting Temptation _____

_____

3. Imprisoned and Forgotten by Man _____

_____

4. Remembered and Promoted by God _____

_____

5. Reaping the Rewards of Righteousness _____

_____

4. Ken Gire, *The Gift of Remembrance* (Grand Rapids, Mich.: Zondervan Publishing House, 1990), pp. 51, 53, 57.

BOOKS FOR PROBING FURTHER

At the beginning of this study, we extended an invitation for you to meet someone—Joseph. In chapter 1 we formally introduced you, and then Joseph's life story quickly took over. You were immediately escorted beyond the acquaintance level, past the casual "How's work?" stage, and into the intensity and openness of intimacy.

It is our hope that you have not simply finished another Bible study but rather gained an invaluable friend, someone whom God can use throughout the rest of your life to tutor you in His sovereignty, grace, and forgiveness.

For those of you who want to continue mining your new relationship with Joseph or some of the issues that our study raised, here are some books we recommend.

Bridges, Jerry. *Trusting God.* Colorado Springs, Colo.: NavPress, 1988. Based on the author's lengthy Bible study on God's sovereignty, this book addresses our Lord's trustworthiness in times of pain. The author's goal is for us to know God better and therefore be able to trust Him more completely—even when life hurts.

Meyer, F. B. *Joseph.* Fort Washington, Pa.: Christian Literature Crusade. In this book, Meyer does a fine job of capturing the emotional nuances of Joseph's pit-to-pinnacle story. Not only do Joseph and his family come alive in these eloquent pages, but the scriptural account shines forth with fresh insight as well.

The Minirth-Meier Clinic West. Forgiveness: The Foundation of Recovery. Newport Beach, Calif.: Minirth-Meier Clinic. Sound cassette series. This series explores the barriers we face in experiencing forgiveness and also explains the practical steps we can take in resolving much of our pain. For a Minirth-Meier tape catalog and order form, write: Minirth-Meier Clinic West, 260 Newport Center Drive, Suite 430, Newport Beach, CA 92660.

Patterson, Ben. *Waiting: Finding Hope When God Seems Silent.* Downers Grove, Ill.: InterVarsity Press, 1989. Ben Patterson writes with compassion and forthrightness about the difficult, sometimes agonizing, experience of waiting. Using the biblical examples of Job and Abraham, he shows us how humility and hope are the keys to enduring these painful times.

Seamands, David A. *Healing of Memories.* Wheaton, Ill.: SP Publications, Victor Books, 1985. In naming his firstborn son Manasseh, Joseph testified to God's graciousness in taking the sting out of his painful memories. In this book, Seamands shows that God's power to heal soul-scarring memories is still available to us today.

Smalley, Gary, and John Trent. *The Blessing.* Nashville, Tenn.: Thomas Nelson Publishers, 1986. In our last lesson we caught only a glimpse of Jacob blessing his grandsons, but this was enough to show that giving a blessing was a significant and meaningful Middle Eastern custom. The life-changing power of this ancient custom is not something limited to biblical times, however. It has the power to alter the course of our lives today, and Gary Smalley and John Trent ably explain how we can successfully apply it.

Smedes, Lewis B. *Forgive and Forget.* New York, N.Y.: Pocket Books, 1984. Smedes writes, "Forgiving seems almost unnatural. Our sense of fairness tells us people should pay for the wrong they do. But forgiving is love's power to break nature's rule." If you would like to model the kind of forgiveness Joseph was able to show his brothers, this book can teach you how.

Swindoll, Charles R. *The Grace Awakening.* Dallas, Tex.: Word Publishing, 1990. It took a supernatural empowering of God's grace for Joseph to forgive his brothers of the terrible things they did to him. If hurts from your past still haunt you, and you look on those relationships with an eye-for-eye, tooth-for-tooth type of vengeance, you need a grace awakening in your life. This latest book by Chuck Swindoll may be just the catalyst you need.

Yancey, Philip. *Disappointment with God.* Grand Rapids, Mich.: Zondervan Publishing House, 1988. As honest, human Christians who do not shrink from the truth, how can we handle those times when we are disappointed by God? Is it irreverent to feel this way, or is it merely being real? In this book, Yancey thoroughly and poignantly explores these issues.

ORDERING INFORMATION

Cassette Tapes and Study Guide

This Bible study guide was designed to be used independently or in conjunction with the broadcast of Chuck Swindoll's taped messages on the topic listed below. If you would like to order cassette tapes or further copies of this study guide, please see the information given below and the Order Form provided on the last page of this guide.

JOSEPH . . . FROM PIT TO PINNACLE

The classic story of a nobody who became somebody, Joseph stands out as a man of remarkable character and integrity. From the lowest level of humanity—slavery—he emerges to the pinnacle of respect. Why? Because he saw Jehovah at work even when he was rejected, misunderstood, falsely accused, and forgotten, and he refused to become resentful and bitter. Joseph's example will challenge you to have a positive, faith-filled attitude when you stand nose-to-nose with broken dreams and seemingly impossible circumstances.

			Calif.*	U.S.	B.C.*	Canada*
JOS	SG	Study Guide	$ 4.20	$ 3.95	$ 5.08	$ 5.08
JOS	CS	Cassette series, includes album cover	36.66	34.50	49.44	46.81
JOS	1–6	Individual cassettes, include messages A and B	5.31	5.00	7.18	6.79

*These prices already include the following charges: for delivery in **California**, 6¼% sales tax; **Canada**, 7% postage and handling; **British Columbia**, 6% British Columbia sales tax (on tapes only) and 7% postage and handling. The prices are subject to change without notice.

JOS 1-A: *Favored Son, Hated Brother*—Genesis 37
       B: *Resisting Temptation*—Genesis 39

JOS 2-A: *Imprisoned and Forgotten by Man*—Genesis 39:20–41:1
       B: *Remembered and Promoted by God*—Genesis 41:1–46

JOS 3-A: *Reaping the Rewards of Righteousness*—Genesis 41:41–57
       B: *Activating a Seared Conscience*—Genesis 42:1–28

JOS 4-A: *Groanings of a Sad Dad*—Genesis 42:29–43:15
     B: *At Last, Together . . . Almost*—Genesis 43:15–34
JOS 5-A: *"I Am Joseph!"*—Genesis 44:1–45:15
     B: *The Ultimate Family Reunion*—Genesis 45:16–46:7, 28–30
JOS 6-A: *Efficiency in Business Then and Now*—Genesis 46:31–47:26
     B: *Highlights of Twilight and Midnight*—Genesis 47:29–31;
        50:15–21

How to Order by Mail

Simply mark on the order form whether you want the series or individual tapes. Mail the form with your payment to the appropriate address listed below. We will process your order as promptly as we can.

United States: Mail your order to the Sales Department at Insight for Living, Post Office Box 4444, Fullerton, California 92634. If you wish your order to be shipped first-class for faster delivery, add 10 percent of the total order amount. Otherwise, please allow four to six weeks for delivery by fourth-class mail. We accept personal checks, money orders, Visa, or MasterCard in payment for materials. Unfortunately, we are unable to offer invoicing or COD orders.

Canada: Mail your order to Insight for Living Ministries, Post Office Box 2510, Vancouver, British Columbia V6B 3W7. Allow approximately four weeks for delivery. We accept personal checks, money orders, Visa, or MasterCard in payment for materials. Unfortunately, we are unable to offer invoicing or COD orders.

Australia, New Zealand, or Papua New Guinea: Mail your order to Insight for Living, Inc., GPO Box 2823 EE, Melbourne, Victoria 3001, Australia. Please allow six to ten weeks for delivery by surface mail. If you would like your order sent airmail, the delivery time may be reduced. Using the United States price as a base, add postage costs—surface or airmail—to the amount of your order. Please use the chart that follows to determine correct postage. Due to fluctuating currency rates, we can accept only personal checks made payable in U.S. funds, international money orders, Visa, or MasterCard in payment for materials.

Overseas: Other overseas residents should mail their orders to our United States office. Please allow six to ten weeks for delivery by surface mail. If you would like your order sent airmail, the delivery time may be reduced. Using the United States price as a base, add postage costs—surface or airmail—to the amount of your order. Please use the chart that follows to determine correct postage. Due to fluctuating currency rates, we can accept only personal checks made payable in U.S. funds, international money orders, Visa, or MasterCard in payment for materials.

Type of Postage	Postage Cost
Surface	10% of total order
Airmail	25% of total order

For Faster Service, Order by Telephone or FAX

For Visa or MasterCard orders, you are welcome to use one of our toll-free numbers between the hours of 8:00 A.M. and 4:30 P.M., Pacific time, Monday through Friday, or our FAX numbers. The numbers to use from anywhere in the United States are **1-800-772-8888** or FAX (714) 773-0932. To order from Canada, call our Vancouver office using **1-800-663-7639** or FAX (604) 596-2975. Vancouver residents, call (604) 596-2910. Australian residents should phone (03) 872-4606. From overseas, call our Sales Department at (714) 870-9161 in the United States.

Our Guarantee

Our cassettes are guaranteed for ninety days against faulty performance or breakage due to a defect in the tape. For best results, please be sure your tape recorder is in good operating condition and is cleaned regularly.

Note: To cover processing and handling, there is a $10 fee for *any* returned check.

Order Form

JOS CS represents the entire *Joseph . . . From Pit to Pinnacle* series in a special album cover, while JOS 1–6 are the individual tapes included in the series. JOS SG represents this study guide, should you desire to order further copies.

Item	Unit Price Calif.*	U.S.	B.C.*	Canada*	Quantity	Amount
JOS CS	$36.66	$34.50	$49.44	$46.81		$
JOS 1	5.31	5.00	7.18	6.79		
JOS 2	5.31	5.00	7.18	6.79		
JOS 3	5.31	5.00	7.18	6.79		
JOS 4	5.31	5.00	7.18	6.79		
JOS 5	5.31	5.00	7.18	6.79		
JOS 6	5.31	5.00	7.18	6.79		
JOS SG	4.20	3.95	5.08	5.08		
					Subtotal	
				Overseas Residents *Pay U.S. price plus 10% surface postage or 25% airmail. Also, see "How to Order by Mail."*		
				U.S. First-Class Shipping *For faster delivery, add 10% for postage and handling.*		
				Gift to Insight for Living *Tax-deductible in the United States and Canada.*		
				Total Amount Due *Please do not send cash.*		$

If there is a balance: ☐ apply it as a donation ☐ please refund
*These prices already include applicable taxes and shipping costs.

Payment by: ☐ Check or money order made payable to Insight for Living or

☐ Credit card (circle one): Visa MasterCard Number _____

Expiration Date _____ Signature _____
We cannot process your credit card purchase without your signature.

Name _____

Address _____

City _____ State/Province _____

Zip/Postal Code _____ Country _____

Telephone ( ) _____ Radio Station ___ ___ ___ ___
If questions arise concerning your order, we may need to contact you.

Mail this order form to the Sales Department at one of these addresses:
Insight for Living, Post Office Box 4444, Fullerton, CA 92634
Insight for Living Ministries, Post Office Box 2510, Vancouver, BC, Canada V6B 3W7
Insight for Living, Inc., GPO Box 2823 EE, Melbourne, VIC 3001, Australia